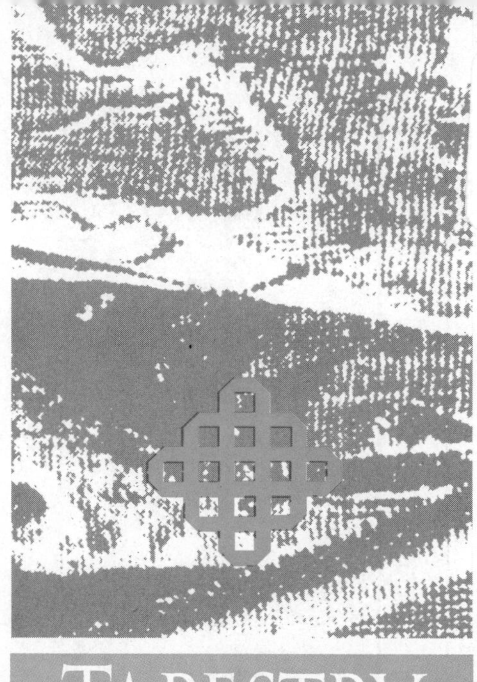

TAPESTRY

GRAMMAR
STRAND 3

TAPESTRY

The **Tapestry** program of language materials is based on the concepts presented in ***The Tapestry of Language Learning:*** *The Individual in the Communicative Classroom* by Robin C. Scarcella & Rebecca L. Oxford.

Each title in this program focuses on:

Individual learner strategies and instruction

The relatedness of skills

Ongoing self-assessment

Authentic material as input

Theme-based learning linked to task-based instruction

Attention to all aspects of communicative competence

TAPESTRY

GRAMMAR STRAND 3

Melanie Schneider

Heinle & Heinle Publishers
An International Thomson
Publishing Company
Boston, Massachusetts, 02116, USA

The publication of *Grammar Strand 3* was directed by the members of the Heinle & Heinle Global Innovations Publishing Team:

David C. Lee, Editorial Director
John F. McHugh, Market Development Director
Lisa J. McLaughlin, Senior Production Services Coordinator

Also participating in the publication of this program were:
Director of Production: Elizabeth Holthaus
Publisher: Stanley J. Galek
Senior Assistant Editor: Kenneth Mattsson
Production Editor: Maryellen Eschmann Killeen
Manufacturing Coordinator: Mary Beth Hennebury
Full Service Project Manager/Compositor: PC&F, Inc.
Art: Dave Blanchette and PC&F, Inc.
Interior Design: Maureen Lauran
Cover Design: Maureen Lauran
Photo/Video Specialist: Jonathan Stark

Manufactured in the United States of America

ISBN: 0-8384-4261-7

Heinle & Heinle Publishers is an International Thomson Publishing Company.

10 9 8 7 6 5 4 3 2 1

To the memory of Robert L. Allen
and to my former ESL students at
the University of Massachusetts, Boston
and elsewhere who have inspired me about
the place of grammar in language learning

PHOTO CREDITS

1, © Gale Zucker/Stock Boston; 16, Courtesy of Ben and Jerry's; 24, 29, © UPI/Bettmann; 27, Reuters/Bettmann; 35, © J. Berndt/Stock Boston; 57, © Peter Menzel/Stock Boston; 75, © Peter Menzel/Stock Boston; 85, Chris Kelley, *Beloit Daily News;* 95, White Buffalo, Inc., Janesville, WI; 103, La Haye Plaza Publications, Inc.; 107, NASA; 123, AP/Wide World; 128, Courtesy of General Mills.

TEXT CREDITS

10, Adapted from Statistics Canada. Used with permission.

15, Rimer, Sara. "Flood Bonds Farmers With Felons, Transforming Them All" (July 29, 1993) *The New York Times.* Copyright © 1993/94 by The New York Times Company. Reprinted by permission.

17, From "Time Line." *Ben & Jerry's Chunk Mail,* 1992. Reprinted by permission.

19, Adapted from *This Is The Body Shop* newsletter, 1994. Used with permission.

22, 23, From the EarthWorks Group, *50 Simple Things You Can Do to Save the Earth,* Berkeley, CA: EarthWorks Press, 1989, p. 62. Used with permission.

23, © Apple Computer, Inc. Used with permission. All rights reserved, Apple® and the Apple logo are registered trademarks of Apple Computer, Inc.

26, 27, Adapted from "Women Managers on Increase in Many Jobs" (Oct. 28, 1992) *Beloit Daily News.* Used by permission.

30, Summers, Dana. Copyright © 1993 by Dana Summers. Reprinted by permission of Tribune Media Services.

32, 33, Peterson, Iver. "Romantics of the Recession Fix Up Their Machine Shop" (July 20, 1993) *The New York Times.* Copyright © 1993/94 by the New York Times Company. Reprinted by permission.

36, From "A New Exercise Alternative? Experts Say They Made a Mistake." *Hope Health Letter,* Dec. 1993. Reprinted with permission, HOPE Publications, Kalamazoo, Michigan, (616) 343-0770.

41, Adapted from Valerie Fahey. "Check Your Emergency IQ." *Health,* July/August 1994. Used with permission.

45, Hofman, Deborah. "For a First-Aid Kit, Forget Caboodle." Copyright © 1993/94 by The New York Times Company. Reprinted by permission.

49, From "Sore Throat Guidelines." *Hope Health Letter,* Dec. 1993. Reprinted with permission, HOPE Publications, Kalamazoo, Michigan, (616) 343-0770.

55, Gott, Peter H. "Here's a Wake-up Call for Snorer" (July 28, 1994) *Beloit Daily News.* Dr. Gott reprinted by permission of Newspaper Enterprise Association, Inc.

60, From "Sorting Mail, Electronically" (June 6, 1994) *The New York Times.* Copyright © 1993/94 by The New York Times Company. Reprinted by permission.

61, Lohr, Steve. "Can E-Mail Cachet = jpmorgan@park.ave?" (June 6, 1994) *The New York Times.* Copyright © 1993/94 by The New York Times Company. Reprinted by permission.

62, Adapted from "FAQs (Frequently Asked Questions)" (July 25, 1994). Copyright © Time, Inc. Used by permission.

63, From "Internet and Online Resources." *Teacher Magazine,* March 1995. Copyright © 1995 Editorial Projects in Education. Ad copy reprinted by permission.

66, "Caller ID Makes Wisconsin Debut." *Ameritech Dialogue in Wisconsin,* July 1994. Ameritech. Reprinted by permission.

67, Adapted from Shelley Emling. "Computers Make Access to Public Records Easy" (Aug. 11, 1994) Reprinted with permission from *The Atlanta Journal* and *The Atlanta Constitution.*

72, America Online® logo. Reprinted by permission.

72, CompuServe® logo. Reprinted by permission.

72, Prodigy® logo. Reprinted by permission.

72, Adapted from Antoinette Martin. "Ultramodern Maturity" (Aug. 14, 1994) *Saint Paul Pioneer Press.* Reprinted by permission of Tribune Media Services.

74, Johnson, Jeff. "Scenarios of People Using the NII [National Information Infrastructure]." *The CPSR Newsletter,* Fall 1994. Copyright © 1994 CPSR. Reprinted by permission. *The CPSR Newsletter* is published quarterly by Computer Professionals for Social Responsiblity, P.O. Box 717, Palo Alto, CA 94302.

80, From "Outlook" (June 6, 1994) *U.S. News & World Report.* Reprinted by permission.

84, Westfeldt, Amy. "Maggie Kuhn, Activist for Elderly, Gray Panther Founder Dies at 89." Copyright © 1995 Associated Press.

85, 86, Cunningham, Kate. "Law and Order: Bilingual Officer Serving as Role Model for City Youth" (March 2, 1995) *Beloit Daily News.* Reprinted by permission.

88, 89, 90, Price, Deb. "U.S. Job Law Needed by Gays and Straights" (May 25, 1994) [Minneapolis] *Star Tribune.* Reprinted by permission of the *Detroit News.*

92, Adapted from "Refrigerator Psychology" (Feb. 4, 1994) *Beloit Daily News.* Used by permission.

94, 95, Adapted from Neal White, "A Modern Day 'Miracle'" (n.d.). Used with permission.

96, 97, Adapted from Neal White, "Looking Horse Family—Keepers of Original Lakota Sacred Pipe" (Sept. 13, 1994) *Beloit Daily News.* Used with permission.

97, 98, 99, Barbieri, Susan. "Thunderbird Woman Lands" (May 28, 1995) *Saint Paul Pioneer Press.* Reprinted by permission.

101, 102, Adapted from "Iowa Man Drives Mower 240 Miles" (Aug. 24, 1994) *Beloit Daily News.* Copyright © 1994 Associated Press.

102, 103, 104, Martell, Chris. "Don't Malign Milwaukee" (Feb. 26, 1995) *Wisconsin State Journal.* Reprinted by permission.

104, 105, Hewlett, Sylvia. "Tough Choices, Great Rewards" (July 17, 1994) *Parade.* Reprinted by permission of the author and *Parade.* Copyright © 1994.

110, Nelan, Bruce W. "Ike's Invasion" (June 6, 1994). Copyright © 1994 Time, Inc. Reprinted by permission.

110, 111, Nelan, Bruce W. "Men Who Fought" (June 6, 1994). Copyright © 1994 Time, Inc. Reprinted by permission.

111, 112, Adapted from Christine Crumbo, "20-Something Important D-Day Facts" (June 5, 1994) *Wisconsin State Journal.* Used with permission of Tribune Media Services.

114, Adapted from Mark Carreau, "25 Years Since Historic Landing" (July 17, 1994) *Wisconsin State Journal.* Copyright © 1994 Houston Chronicle Publishing Company. Used with permission.

118, Adapted from Mark Carreau, "When Will Humans Return" (July 17, 1994) *Wisconsin State Journal.* Copyright © 1994 Houston Chronicle Publishing Company. Used with permission.

124, Giscard d'Estaing, Valerie-Ann and Mark Young (Eds.). "The Prometheus System" from *Inventions and Discoveries 1993.* New York: Facts on File, 1993. Reprinted by permission.

125, Giscard d'Estaing, Valerie-Ann and Mark Young (Eds.). "Antisense Polygalacturonase (PG) Gene" from *Inventions and Discoveries 1993.* New York: Facts on File, 1993. Reprinted by permission.

126, Forman, Craig. "Totem in Tokyo" (April 24, 1995) *Wall Street Journal.* Copyright © 1995 Dow Jones & Company, Inc. Reprinted by permission.

126, 127, Giscard d'Estaing, Valerie-Ann and Mark Young (Eds.), "The Tantrum Brick' from *Inventions and Discoveries 1993.* New York: Facts on File, 1993. Reprinted by permission.

127, Roylston, Robert M. "Post-its" from *Serendipity: Accidental Discoveries in Science.* New York: John Wiley & Sons, Inc., 1989. Reprinted by permission. Post-it® is a registered trademark of 3M.

131, 132, Warner, Fara. "Imperfect Picture" (April 24, 1995) *Wall Street Journal.* Copyright © 1995 Dow Jones & Company, Inc. Reprinted by permission.

133, "34 Million Americans Have Reached 65th Birthday" (April 27, 1995) *Beloit Daily News.* Copyright © 1995 Associated Press. Reprinted by permission.

137, No title [definitions of six political systems] (June 27, 1993) *Wisconsin State Journal.* Copyright © 1993 Knight Ridder, Inc. Reprinted by permission of Tribune Media Services.

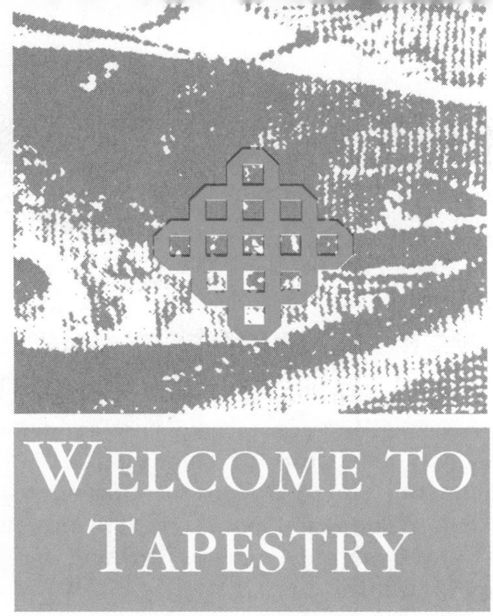

Welcome to Tapestry

Enter the world of Tapestry! Language learning can be seen as an ever-developing tapestry woven with many threads and colors. The elements of the tapestry are related to different language skills like listening and speaking, reading and writing; the characteristics of the teachers; the desires, needs, and backgrounds of the students; and the general second language development process. When all these elements are working together harmoniously, the result is a colorful, continuously growing tapestry of language competence of which the student and the teacher can be proud.

This volume is part of the Tapestry Program for students of English as a second language (ESL) at levels from beginning to "bridge" (which follows the advanced level and prepares students to enter regular postsecondary programs along with native English speakers). Upper level materials in the Tapestry Program are also appropriate for developmental English courses—especially reading and composition courses. Tapestry levels include:

Beginning
Low Intermediate
High Intermediate
Advanced
High Advanced
Bridge

Because the Tapestry Program provides a unified theoretical and pedagogical foundation for all its components, you can optimally use all the Tapestry student books in a coordinated fashion as an entire curriculum of materials. (They will be published from 1993 to 1996 with further editions likely thereafter.) Alternatively, you can decide to use just certain Tapestry volumes, depending on your specific needs.

Tapestry is primarily designed for ESL students at postsecondary institutions in North America. Some want to learn ESL for academic or career advancement, others for social and personal reasons. Tapestry builds directly on all these motivations. Tapestry stimulates learners to do their best. It enables learners to use English naturally and to develop fluency as well as accuracy.

Tapestry Principles

The following principles underlie the instruction provided in all of the components of the Tapestry Program.

EMPOWERING LEARNERS

Language learners in Tapestry classrooms are active and increasingly responsible for developing their English language skills and related cultural abilities. This self direction leads to better, more rapid learning. Some cultures virtually train their students to be passive in the classroom, but Tapestry weans them from passivity by providing exceptionally high interest materials, colorful and motivating activities, personalized self-reflection tasks, peer tutoring and other forms of cooperative learning, and powerful learning strategies to boost self direction in learning.

The empowerment of learners creates refreshing new roles for teachers, too. The teacher serves as facilitator, co-communicator, diagnostician, guide, and helper. Teachers are set free to be more creative at the same time their students become more autonomous learners.

HELPING STUDENTS IMPROVE THEIR LEARNING STRATEGIES

Learning strategies are the behaviors or steps an individual uses to enhance his or her learning. Examples are taking notes, practicing, finding a conversation partner, analyzing words, using background knowledge, and controlling anxiety. Hundreds of such strategies have been identified. Successful language learners use language learning strategies that are most effective for them given their particular learning style, and they put them together smoothly to fit the needs of a given language task. On the other hand, the learning strategies of less successful learners are a desperate grab-bag of ill-matched techniques.

All learners need to know a wide range of learning strategies. All learners need systematic practice in choosing and applying strategies that are relevant for various learning needs. Tapestry is one of the only ESL programs that overtly weaves a comprehensive set of learning strategies into language activities in all its volumes. These learning strategies are arranged in eight broad categories throughout the Tapestry books:

Forming Concepts
Personalizing
Remembering New Material
Managing Your Learning
Understanding and Using Emotions
Overcoming Limitations
Testing Hypotheses
Learning with Others

The most useful strategies are sometimes repeated and flagged with a note, "It Works! Learning Strategy . . ." to remind students to use a learning strategy they have already encountered. This recycling reinforces the value of learning strategies and provides greater practice.

RECOGNIZING AND HANDLING LEARNING STYLES EFFECTIVELY

Learners have different learning styles (for instance, visual, auditory, hands-on; reflective, impulsive; analytic, global; extroverted, introverted; closure-oriented, open). Particularly in an ESL setting, where students come from vastly different cultural backgrounds, learning styles differences abound and can cause "style conflicts."

Unlike most language instruction materials, Tapestry provides exciting activities specifically tailored to the needs of students with a large range of learning styles. You can use any Tapestry volume with the confidence that the activities and materials are intentionally geared for many different styles. Insights from the latest educational and psychological research undergird this style-nourishing variety.

OFFERING AUTHENTIC, MEANINGFUL COMMUNICATION

Students need to encounter language that provides authentic, meaningful communication. They must be involved in real-life communication tasks that cause them to *want* and *need* to read, write, speak, and listen to English. Moreover, the tasks—to be most effective—must be arranged around themes relevant to learners.

Themes like family relationships, survival in the educational system, personal health, friendships in a new country, political changes, and protection of the environment are all valuable to ESL learners. Tapestry focuses on topics like these. In every Tapestry volume, you will see specific content drawn from very broad areas such as home life, science and technology, business, humanities, social sciences, global issues, and multiculturalism. All the themes are real and important, and they are fashioned into language tasks that students enjoy.

At the advanced level, Tapestry also includes special books each focused on a single broad theme. For instance, there are two books on business English, two on English for science and technology, and two on academic communication and study skills.

UNDERSTANDING AND VALUING DIFFERENT CULTURES

Many ESL books and programs focus completely on the "new" culture, that is, the culture which the students are entering. The implicit message is that ESL students should just learn about this target culture, and there is no need to understand their own culture better or to find out about the cultures of their international classmates. To some ESL students, this makes them feel their own culture is not valued in the new country.

Tapestry is designed to provide a clear and understandable entry into North American culture. Nevertheless, the Tapestry Program values *all* the cultures found in the ESL classroom. Tapestry students have constant opportunities to become "culturally fluent" in North American culture while they are learning English, but they also have the chance to think about the cultures of their classmates and even understand their home culture from different perspectives.

INTEGRATING THE LANGUAGE SKILLS

Communication in a language is not restricted to one skill or another. ESL students are typically expected to learn (to a greater or lesser degree) all four language skills: reading, writing, speaking, and listening. They are also expected to develop strong grammatical competence, as well as becoming socioculturally sensitive and knowing what to do when they encounter a "language barrier."

Research shows that multi-skill learning is more effective than isolated-skill learning, because related activities in several skills provide reinforcement and refresh the learner's memory. Therefore, Tapestry integrates all the skills. A given Tapestry volume might highlight one skill, such as reading, but all other skills are also included to support and strengthen overall language development.

However, many intensive ESL programs are divided into classes labeled according to one skill (Reading Comprehension Class) or at most two skills (Listening/Speaking Class or Oral Communication Class). The volumes in the Tapestry Program can easily be used to fit this traditional format, because each volume clearly identifies its highlighted or central skill(s).

Grammar is interwoven into all Tapestry volumes. However, there is also a separate reference book for students, *The Tapestry Grammar,* and a Grammar Strand composed of grammar "work-out" books at each of the levels in the Tapestry Program.

Other Features of the Tapestry Program

PILOT SITES

It is not enough to provide volumes full of appealing tasks and beautiful pictures. Users deserve to know that the materials have been pilot-tested. In many ESL series, pilot testing takes place at only a few sites or even just in the classroom of the author. In contrast, Heinle & Heinle Publishers have developed a network of Tapestry Pilot Test Sites throughout North America. At this time, there are approximately 40 such sites, although the number grows weekly. These sites try out the materials and provide suggestions for revisions. They are all actively engaged in making Tapestry the best program possible.

AN OVERALL GUIDEBOOK

To offer coherence to the entire Tapestry Program and especially to offer support for teachers who want to understand the principles and practice of Tapestry, we have written a book entitled, *The Tapestry of Language Learning. The Individual in the Communicative Classroom* (Scarcella and Oxford, published in 1992 by Heinle & Heinle).

A Last Word

We are pleased to welcome you to Tapestry! We use the Tapestry principles every day, and we hope these principles—and all the books in the Tapestry Program—provide you the same strength, confidence, and joy that they give us. We look forward to comments from both teachers and students who use any part of the Tapestry Program.

Rebecca L. Oxford
University of Alabama
Tuscaloosa, Alabama

Robin C. Scarcella
University of California at Irvine
Irvine, California

WEAVING THE GRAMMAR STRANDS INTO THE TAPESTRY SERIES

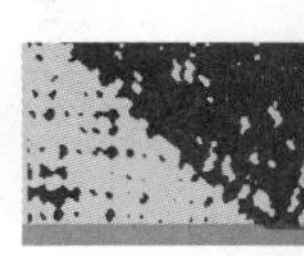

Grammar Strands is a five-level grammar series in the Tapestry Program. These materials are designed to supplement any course in which grammar is needed to address the specific needs of learners. The work-text format allows for greater flexibility for both in-class and out-of-class use. *Grammar Strand 1* and *Grammar Strand 2* feature a complete and comprehensive presentation of structures while *Grammar Strand 3, 4,* and *5* may be supplemented with *The Tapestry Grammar,* the Tapestry Program grammar reference, for a more in-depth study. The grammatical content for the Grammar Strands books was selected on the basis of needs of students at the proficiency levels covered by particular books and also on the basis of grammar issues raised in other materials at that level.

Their title reveals the purpose of the Grammar Strands in the Tapestry series: a focus on English grammar that is woven throughout the Tapestry materials making grammar one strand of thread interwoven with many other strands of language study. This approach to language learning enriches the study of grammar by putting it into context of learning to communicate in English—rather than learning linguistic facts about English. Learning English grammar in context is a fundamental aspect of the "tapestry of language" that is contained in this coherent series of materials.

While these books differ from the other books in the Tapestry series because of this focus on grammar, they take the same approach to language learning. The Grammar Strands have thematic unity through presentation of grammar in the context of particular themes that run through a chapter. The students work with authentic language in authentic contexts. In addition, information about and practice with learning strategies is embedded throughout each of the Grammar Strands. While these books are focused on issues in English grammar, they also help students to become more skillful in all areas of language learning.

Grammar Strands at Levels 1 and 2

At levels 1 and 2, the Grammar Strands are complete grammar textbooks that can be used with other Tapestry materials or alone as the complete text for a lower proficiency level grammar course.

To provide for the needs of students at levels 1 and 2, more explanatory material is included than in the Grammar Strands at the upper levels. The grammar explanations given in *Grammar Strand 1* and *2* are based on the same approach used in *The Tapestry Grammar* and prepare students for the use of that reference when they reach the appropriate proficiency level. In *Grammar Strand 1* and *2,* terminology and explanations are presented, however, in language and examples more appropriate to the communication skills of students at the lower proficiency levels. As a result of having more explanatory materials in addition to a full range of examples and exercises, *Grammar Strand 1* and *2* are somewhat longer than *Grammar Strand 3, 4,* and *5.*

Teachers who work with students at these lower proficiency levels will find *Grammar Strand 1* and *2* wonderful new resources. All too often, materials at this level provide either too much grammar and not enough communication—or random communication activities that do not provide a coherent understanding of how English works. These grammar books are a useful balance of communication with grammar study. Moreover, they treat the lower proficiency students with respect and provide content that is worthy of adult learners. As part of a total series of materials, *Grammar Strand 1* and *2* can be used to help students move in a coherent sequence to higher levels of proficiency in English.

Grammar Strands at Levels 3, 4, and 5

At levels 3, 4, and 5, the Grammar Strands are grammar workbooks designed to be used with the reading, writing, listening, speaking, and/or culture books in the Tapestry series. For example, in a course that combines reading with grammar, the teacher can use the appropriate Tapestry reading book along with the Grammar Strand for that proficiency level. This approach to grammar materials is another example of the innovative design developed for the Tapestry series. While the grammatical explanations and terminology come from *The Tapestry Grammar,* the Grammar Strands are not designed to be used as a supplement for this reference text. Rather than providing materials that would have students focus on grammar in isolation, the Tapestry approach has led to the development of these Grammar Strands that can be woven into classes that are focused on communication and on content.

Explanations, Examples, and Exercises

THE BALANCE IN *GRAMMAR STRANDS* 3, 4, AND 5

All grammar textbooks are built on various combinations of the three "E's"—explanations, examples, and exercises. At levels 3, 4, and 5, the Grammar Strands are true workbooks, emphasizing the exercises and examples rather than the explanations. Cross references are provided to the relevant sections of *The Tapestry Grammar* for students and teachers who would like more grammatical explanation. At these upper levels, the Grammar Strands provide supplementary and complementary learning activities rather than additional discussion of the grammar topic. For a more complete grammar course, or for the richest possible combination of materials, a teacher will include *The Tapestry Grammar* in the selection of textbooks for courses using the Grammar Strands at levels 3, 4, and 5.

Patricia Byrd
Department of Applied Linguistics and ESL
Georgia State University

PREFACE

Grammar Strand 3 is a grammar text for high-intermediate ESL students. It is designed to be used as a supplement to other texts, for example, the reading, writing, listening, speaking and/or culture books in the Tapestry series, and as a complement to *The Tapestry Grammar.* In keeping with the theme-based nature of the Tapestry series, each of the six chapters of the book focuses on a theme: The Working World, Health Issues, The Information Superhighway, Lifestyles, Anniversaries, and The Post-War World. Because the explanations, readings, and activities in each lesson relate to a particular theme, the grammar topics in each lesson are contextualized and reinforced.

The 24 lessons in *Grammar Strand 3* do not, with few exceptions, introduce new structures to high-intermediate ESL students. Instead, they provide practice in areas of grammar that are often problematic for intermediate-level learners. The text begins by introducing 16 grammatical terms from *The Tapestry Grammar* that are used throughout the workbook. Students and teachers who are unfamiliar with these terms may refer to *The Tapestry Grammar* for additional explanation. The grammar topics and structures in *Grammar Strand 3* generally move from words and phrases (Chapters 1, 2, 3, 4) to sentences (Chapter 5), and then to discourse (Chapter 6). However, since the book includes many authentic materials from other sources, these grammar points are previewed and practiced in a discourse context. Many of the grammar topics and structures in *Grammar Strand 3* appear again in expanded form in *Grammar Strands 4* and *5*.

Chapter Features

The lessons in each chapter are divided into three sections: Preview, Presentation, and Practice (grammar-related activities). Learning strategies are interspersed throughout each lesson.

LEARNING STRATEGIES

The Tapestry approach emphasizes the acquisition of skills to improve learning. Each lesson identifies useful learning strategies and then applies them in the activities that follow. The purpose of these strategies is to remind learners of tools they already have that can enhance their ability to learn.

PREVIEW

The Preview highlights a grammar topic or structure and encourages learners to think about what they know about it. Through questions, short passages, charts, tables, illustrations, or a combination of these, the Preview sets the scene for a theme or topic that continues throughout the lesson.

PRESENTATION

The Presentation briefly explains the grammar topic that is featured in each lesson. Intentionally short, these explanations often include tables or charts that summarize key points. For further explanation, please refer to a grammar reference text or to corresponding chapters of The Tapestry Grammar, as outlined below.

Grammar Strand 3 LESSON	*The Tapestry Grammar* CHAPTER
1. Kinds of Verbs: Simple, regular and irregular, auxiliaries, expanded	Chapters 1, 8
2. Verb Endings: Simple present and BE (am/are/is) + -ing (Present, Progressive)	Chapter 8
3. Verb Endings: Simple past and BE (was/were) + -ing (Past Progressive)	Chapter 8
4. BE + -d/t/n (Passive Voice)	Chapter 9
5. HAVE (have/has) + -d/t/n (Present Perfect)	Chapter 8
6. Had + -d/t/n (Past Perfect)	Chapter 8
7. Expressing Ability, and Making General Requests, Predictions, and Inferences	Chapter 8
8. Expressing Permission, Recommendation, and Obligation	Chapter 8
9. Expressing Real Expectations and Imagined Situations in the Present (*If* Clauses)	Chapter 8
10. Verbs Followed Only by to + Base or -ing	Chapters 10, 11
11. Verbs Followed by to + Base or -ing	Chapters 10, 11
12. Verbs Followed by "Subject" + Verbal Phrase	Chapter 11
13. An Overview: Simple and Expanded Noun Phrases	Chapters 5, 6
14. Simple Noun Phrases: Definite, indefinite, and zero article, the other/another/other + noun	Chapter 5
15. Simple Noun Phrases: Definite/Indefinite quantifiers + noun	Chapter 5
16. *Wh-* Clauses: Relative clauses as postmodifiers	Chapter 6
17. Choosing the Right Article: *the, a/an,* or zero article	Chapters 5, 6
18. Parallel Structure: Words, phrases, and clauses	Chapter 14
19. Ties Within Sentences: Coordinators and subordinators	Chapter 4
20. Ties Within Sentences: Pronouns in affirmative and negative sentences	Chapters 5, 7
21. Ties Across Sentences: Articles, other determiners, and pronouns	Chapters 5, 7
22. Ties Across Sentences: Repetitions and transition words	Chapter 4
23. Asking Questions: An overview of question types	Chapter 2
24. Asking Questions: Full and reduced forms	Chapter 2

PRACTICE

The practice activities make up the major part of the workbook. These activities are designed to reinforce what students already know or have learned in the Presentation sections. They vary in type of activity (fill in the blank/cloze exercises, short answers, sentences, dialogues, paragraphs or brief essay), student grouping (individual, partner, group), and language skill (speaking, listening, reading, writing). Although some of the activities are sequential, many are not. Students and teachers are encouraged to skim the activities in each lesson and choose those that are most useful.

To build interest, authentic materials related to the chapter theme are included in the activities. When the reading passages from these materials are challenging, unfamiliar vocabulary items are highlighted and briefly defined after the passage. In addition, occasional For Your Information sections provide background knowledge or cultural information needed to understand the readings fully or complete the activities. Teachers, who know their students best, are invited to add their own cultural notes as needed.

Acknowledgments

Many people provided invaluable assistance and encouragement to me as I wrote and revised this text. I am grateful to Patricia Werner for introducing me to the Tapestry series and encouraging me to become an author. *The Tapestry Grammar* authors Alice Deakins, Kate Parry, and Robert Viscount as well as "grammar guru" Patricia Byrd deserve special mention for their thoughtful and helpful discussions about the *Grammar Strand* books, especially early in their development. I am also grateful to four anonymous reviewers, whose insightful comments and suggestions have made *Grammar Strand 3* a better book. Likewise, I would like to thank my *Grammar Strand* colleagues, especially Melissa Derr, University of Findley, and Nancy Herzfeld-Pipkin, San Diego State University, for taking time to talk through many questions and review parts of the manuscript.

I would also like to thank Cheryl Benz (Miami-Dade Community College), Kim Brown (Portland State University), Sally Gearheart (Santa Rosa Community College), Mary Hill-Shinn (El Paso Community College), Helen Huntley (West Virginia University), Michael Knepp (Texas Intensive English Program), Lynne Nickerson (Dekalb College) and Mary Wood (Kansas State University) for their helpful comments during the development of this manuscript.

Many thanks go to Ken Mattsson and David Lee at Heinle & Heinle for their ongoing support, guidance, and helpful suggestions throughout the writing process. Elaine Hall helped see me through the challenging final stages of the book while it was in production. In many ways, this book is a tribute to the experience and good humor of these three people. Finally, I gratefully acknowledge the support and editing skills of my husband, Paul Campbell, who weathered the trying moments and is as happy as I am that the book is completed.

Melanie Schneider

CONTENTS

5 *Language in Context: Sentences* *107*

6 *Language in Context: Discourse* *123*

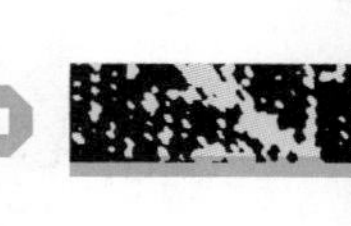

There are 16 grammatical terms that will help you understand and use the explanations and practice activities in the Grammar Strand books:

adjective	preposition
adverbial	prepositional phrase
auxiliary verb	pronoun
expanded verb	subject
independent (main) clause	subordinate clause
noun	subordinator
noun phrase	verb
predicate	verbal phrase

The following table lists these 16 basic terms and gives examples of each. The same terms are introduced in Chapter 1 of *The Tapestry Grammar* and are explained in more detail throughout the book.

TABLE 1 SUMMARY OF 16 BASIC TERMS

PRIMARY POSITIONS	EXAMPLES
Subjects	**I** sometimes question myself. **English** was one of the main subjects at school. **My first experience with English** started in junior high school.
Predicates	I **sometimes question myself.** English **was one of the main subjects at school.** My first experience with English **started in junior high school.**
Adverbials	are groups of words that usually occur before the subject, after the predicate, or before the (main) verb: Sentence adverbials: **When I look back**, I question myself. I question myself **when I look back.** Adverbials with verbs: I **often** forgot everything. I was **totally** discouraged.
WORDS AND PHRASES	
Nouns	Singular: **teacher; woman; experience; education** Plural: **teachers; women; experiences**
Noun Phrases	**our teachers** **women like me** **my first experience with English** **English education**
Pronouns	can replace **nouns** or **noun phrases** they we it

	Subject Position		*Object Position*	
	Singular	Plural	Singular	Plural
	I	**we**	**me**	**us**
	you	**you**	**you**	**you**
	he/she/it	**they**	**him/her/it**	**them**

Adjectives	are single words or groups of words that describe a **noun:** an **unknown** world the outdated education system My **first English** lesson was **easy.**

Verbs (simple) consist of one word that has tense; simple regular verbs end in the base alone, the base + **-s**, or the base + **-ed**:

I **remember** that day well, and my mother **does** too.
After flying more than seven hours, we finally **landed** in Madrid.
Madrid **looked** like New York, but it **sounded** different.

Expanded Verbs are **verbs** preceded by one or more **auxiliary verbs:**

didn't learn
was confused
had been answering
will have

Auxiliary Verbs begin all **expanded verbs** and are divided into four groups: DO, BE, HAVE, and the modals. Only the first **auxiliary** shows tense and agrees with the subject:

	Type of Auxiliary
I **didn't** learn everything in my first six months in Japan.	DO
At first, I **was** confused by hearing *yes* (*hai*) when it meant *no.*	BE
Some people **had been** answering my questions politely instead of honestly.	HAVE, BE
I **will** have to change how I ask questions.	Modal

Verbals and Verbal Phrases consist of **verbs** that do not have tense; **verbals** take the form of (*to*) + base, base + *-ing,* or base + *-d/t/n:*

Verbal Phrase

Verbal +	*rest of phrase*
to handle	**all the customers**
working	**as a cashier**
located	**on 34th Street and 6th Avenue**

Prepositions and Prepositional Phrases **Prepositions** begin **prepositional phrases** and are usually followed by a noun **phrase** or a **verbal phrase:**

Prepositional Phrase

Preposition +	*noun/verbal phrase*
for	**eight years**
in	**the English language**
by	**working hard**
instead of	**memorizing facts**

CLAUSES

Independent (main) Clauses consist of at least one **subject** and one **predicate;** they can stand alone as a sentence:

Subject	*Predicate*
The Ursuline Convent	**is a boarding school in the U.K.**
I	**went there to finish my education.**
Every boarder	**had to bring up her luggage to her room.**

Subordinate Clause consist of at least one **subject** and one **predicate,** but they *can't* stand alone as a sentence:

When I was a young girl, I attended the Ursuline Convent School in the U.K. At first I didn't like to talk much **because my English was so poor.** I remember **that the sisters were patient with me.**

Subordinators are words that introduce a **subordinate clause:**

Subordinate Clause

Subordinator +	*Clause*
when	**I was a young girl**
because	**my English was so poor**
that	**the sisters were patient with me**

CHAPTER 1

Verbs

Lesson 1: Kinds of Verbs

Simple verbs, regular and irregular verbs, auxiliaries, and expanded verbs

PREVIEW

1. **Test your knowledge**. Do you know the following kinds of verbs? Check "Yes" or "No" for each verb. Then give an example of those you checked "Yes."

	YES	NO	EXAMPLE
a. simple verb	____	____	____________________
b. regular verb	____	____	____________________
c. irregular verb	____	____	____________________
d. auxiliary	____	____	____________________
e. expanded verb	____	____	____________________

2. **Partners.** Compare your answers in (1) above. Then read the following job ads. With a partner, underline examples of simple verbs (S), auxiliary verbs (A), and expanded verbs (E). To help you begin, these verbs are underlined in example (a). Write the letter referring to the verb (S, A, or E) next to each underlined verb.

a.

MARKETING

No degree, no experience, no problem! National marketing firm is expanding throughout the California area. If you like working with major league sports, golf, or the entertainment industry, call 647-4321 to set up an interview. **Internships and summer help available!**

b.

SALES REPRESENTATIVE

Future 50 Company seeks business consultant with minimum three yrs. successful outside sales experience. Preferred candidates will have dealt with company owners and managers. Solution oriented, goal driven, assertive, and self-managed are ideal qualifications. Current sales staff are earning $60–80,000. Excellent benefit plan including health, 401K, and profit sharing. Qualified applicants should send a resume in confidence to: P.O. 01234, Santa Cruz, CA 95062.

c.

PROGRAMMER/ANALYST

Bayview Clinic has a full-time position for a Programmer/Analyst. Candidates must possess a four-year degree from an accredited college—prefer a computer science major. We prefer experience in UNIX and C++. Strong oral and written skills are required. Qualified candidates should send their resume in confidence to: Employment Generalist, Bayview Clinic, Seaside, CA 93955.

PRESENTATION

Simple verbs, regular verbs, irregular verbs, auxiliaries, and expanded verbs are five kinds of verbs that occur in sentences. Table 1.1 summarizes these verbs and gives examples of each.

TABLE 1.1 Types of Verbs

VERB	SHORT DEFINITION		
Simple verbs	consist of only one word. show tense, the time a sentence refers to. have three forms: **1.** The **base** form of the verb (work) **2.** The **base** + **-s** or (works) **3.** The **base** + **-ed** (worked)		
Regular verbs	add **-ed,** or less often, **-d** to the **base** in the past. (rent → rent**ed,** manage → manag**ed**)		
Irregular verbs	do *not* take the **-ed** ending in the past. change spelling in the past:	**Base**	**Past**
	1. vowel change	eat write	ate wrote
	2. consonant change	send build	sent built
	3. vowel + consonant change	do sleep	did slept
	4. complete change	be go	was/were went
	5. no change (only a few verbs)	put set	put set
Auxiliaries	come from one of four groups: (1) BE group, (2) DO group, (3) HAVE group, and (4) MODAL group. occur with another verb in a complete sentence. They'<u>re</u> <u>looking</u> for an apartment. (BE) They <u>don't</u> <u>want</u> one on the first floor. (DO) They <u>haven't been</u> <u>looking</u> for long. (HAVE + BE) They <u>should</u> <u>find</u> one soon. (MODAL)		
Expanded verbs	consist of one or more **auxiliaries** and the verb itself (is working, may have worked). are sometimes called verb phrases.		

For more information about kinds of verbs, see *The Tapestry Grammar,* Chapters 1, 8, and 9.)

PRACTICE

Activity 1
Read the chart and the passage that follows. Then answer the questions.

FIGURE 1.1

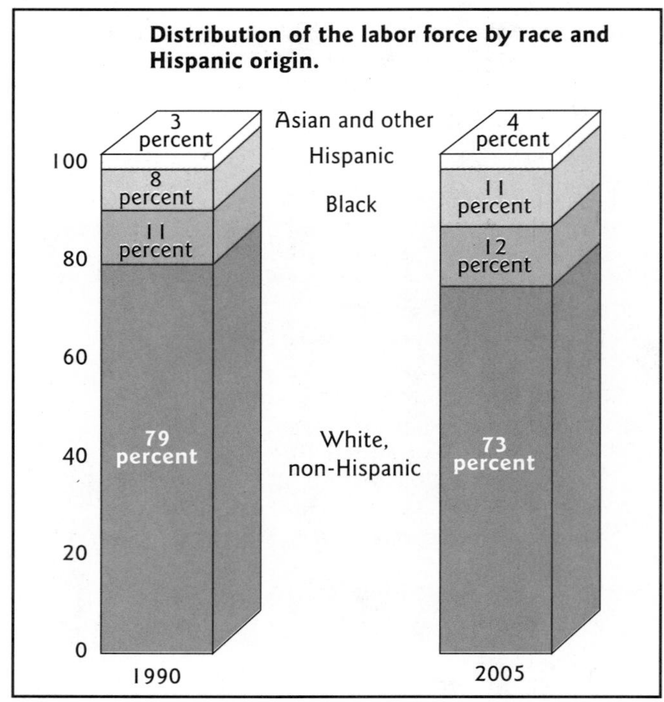

Source: U.S. Bureau of Labor Statistics, "Tomorrow's Jobs," in the *Occuptional Outlook Handbook.* Washington, DC: U.S. Department of Labor, 1992–93.

TRENDS IN THE U.S. LABOR FORCE

Population is the single most important factor affecting the size and composition of the labor force, which includes people who are working or looking for work. The U.S. civilian labor force totaled 125 million in 1990 and is expected to reach 151 million by 2005. This projected increase—21 percent—represents a slowdown in both the number added to the labor force and the rate of growth, largely because of slower population growth.

America's workers will be an increasingly diverse group as it approaches the year 2005. White non-Hispanic men will make up a smaller share of the labor force, and women and minority group members will comprise a larger proportion than in 1990. Historically, white non-Hispanics have been the largest component of the labor force, but their share has been dropping. It is expected to drop from 79 percent of the labor force in 1990 to 73 percent by 2005. Hispanics will add about 7 million workers to the labor force from 1990 to 2005, an increase of 75 percent. In spite of this dramatic growth, Hispanics' share of the labor force will only increase from 8 to 11 percent, as Figure 1.1 shows. The percentage of black workers is expected to increase only slightly, from 11 percent to 12 percent.

The number of women in the labor force will increase faster than the total labor force, but more slowly than between 1975 and 1990. Women made up only 40 percent of the labor force in 1975; by 2005 they are expected to constitute 47 percent.

Slightly adapted from the U.S. Department of Labor, Bureau of Labor Statistics, "Tomorrow's Jobs," Washington, DC: U.S. Government Printing Office, in *Occupational Outlook Handbook,* 1992–1993.

1. In paragraph 1, **simple verbs** are underlined. Recall that simple verbs consist of only one word and show **tense,** the **time** the sentence refers to. They do this by sometimes adding an ending onto the **base** form of the verb: -s for third person singular (he/she/it) in the present tense and -ed for regular verbs in the past. Circle the **present tense verbs** and put a box around the **past tense verbs** in paragraph 1.

   a. How many **present tense verbs** are there? ________________

   b. How many **past tense verbs** are there? ________________

2. In paragraph 2, **expanded verbs** are underlined. Expanded verbs always consist of at least one **auxiliary** and the verb itself. Only the first auxiliary of an expanded verb carries the tense.

   a. Which **expanded verb** has two **auxiliaries**? ______________________

   b. List all the other **auxiliaries** in paragraph 2. ______________________

   ____

3. a. In paragraph 3, the verbs are not underlined. There is one example of a **simple verb.** Can you find it? ______________________

   b. In the same paragraph, there are two examples of **expanded verbs**. Can you find them? ______________________

Activity 2

Partners. Read the passage and then answer the questions that follow. Compare your answers with your partner's.

EARNING POWER

(1) In 1992, Shaquille O'Neal, a 7-foot 1-inch basketball player, signed a seven-year $39.9 million contract with the Orlando Magic. (2) Since 1993, late-night TV talk show host David Letterman has received $14 million a year for switching channels from **NBC** to **CBS.** (3) In comparison, Bill Clinton has collected a relatively modest $200,000 a year as President of the United States. (4) But compared to those he has governed, Clinton is still in the top 1 percent of American earners.

(5) According to the Bureau of Labor Statistics, the **median wage** for U.S. workers was $23,140 in 1992. (6) This wage was 3.4 percent higher than in 1991, but with an **inflation** rate of 3.2 percent, workers earned only slightly more. (7) Women, however, have continued to **gain** in earning power. (8) In 1992, they made an average of $19,812 compared to $26,260 for men. (9) That's 75.5 cents for every $1.00 males earned, an increase of 1.5 cents from 1991. (10) In comparison, blacks earned 77.5 cents and Hispanics 70 cents for every $1.00 earned by whites.

Adapted from Michael VerMeulen, "What People Earn," *Parade,* June 20, 1993.

NBC, CBS major TV networks
median wage average amount of money earned; 50 percent earn more and 50 percent earn less
inflation rising prices for goods and services
gain go up, increase

1. Circle all the simple verb forms in the passage, "Earning Power." How many *different* simple verbs did you find? Don't count the same verb in its past or present form as different.
2. Underline all the expanded verb forms.
3. Put a box around all the auxiliary verbs.

NOTE When the verb be occurs alone, it is not an auxiliary verb.

Activity 3

Because of the cost of advertising, job ads are often written in short phrases and incomplete sentences. Expand the following job ads so that each sentence has a subject and a main verb (a verb that shows tense). Remember that in imperative sentences (e.g., "Call 459-4321"), the subject is understood to be you, so you don't need to add it. You may want to combine some phrases into one sentence.

1. **ART DEPARTMENT ASSISTANT**—Part-time help needed in Art Department of screen printing company. Darkroom experience helpful. Call 459-4321.

____

____

____

____

____

2. **HOTEL FRONT DESK**—Self-starter needed for part-time second shift position. Must have computer skills. Neat appearance. Good diction. Apply in person 9–11 A.M. or 3–5 P.M. weekdays at 1007 N. Bass St.

____

____

____

____

____

____

3. **BAKER**—Professional baker. Clean work environment. Experience necessary. Own transportation a must. 3rd shift. Good pay. Resume or applications at Best Baking Co., Santa Cruz, CA 95062

____

____

____

____

____

____

4. **COLLECTIONS FINANCIAL OFFICE**—Reliable people with good speaking ability. (Bilingual) English/Spanish helpful, but not required. Full- and part-time, flexible hours. Will train. Call Randy between 9 A.M.–1 P.M., 427-8910.

____

____

____

____

____

____

Lesson 2: Verb Endings

Simple Present and BE (am/are/is) + -ing (present progressive)

PREVIEW

Many employers require job interviews before they hire new employees. How do you prepare for and behave at a job interview? If you haven't had a job before, how do you plan to prepare for one in the future? Circle the number next to each statement that best describes your behavior.

1	2	3	4	5
Never true for me	Rarely true for me	Sometimes true for me	Often true for me	Always true for me

1. I learn as much as possible about the organization.	1	2	3	4	5
2. I have a specific job or jobs in mind.	1	2	3	4	5
3. I prepare answers to general questions about myself.	1	2	3	4	5
4. I practice an interview with a friend or relative.	1	2	3	4	5
5. I arrive before the scheduled time of my interview.	1	2	3	4	5
6. I dress more conservatively than usual.	1	2	3	4	5
7. I chew gum and smoke.	1	2	3	4	5
8. I answer each question promptly and concisely.	1	2	3	4	5
9. I learn the name of my interviewer and shake hands as we meet.	1	2	3	4	5
10. I use proper language and avoid slang.	1	2	3	4	5
11. I answer questions, but I don't ask any.	1	2	3	4	5
12. I thank the interviewer after the interview.	1	2	3	4	5
13. I send the interviewer a follow-up letter.	1	2	3	4	5

All 13 statements are in the **present tense.** Can you give a reason why?

____

____

PRESENTATION

Simple present (base/base + -s). The simple present tense has two forms: **base** and **base + -s.** Third person, singular subjects (**he, she, it**) take the **base + -s** form. All other subjects take the **base** form, as Table 1.2 shows.

TABLE 1.2 Forming the Present Tense (**base/base + -s**)

STATEMENT		NEGATIVE			QUESTION		
I You We They	listen.	I You We They	do not don't	listen.	Do	I you we they	listen?
She He It	listens.	She He It	does not doesn't	listen.	Does	she he it	listen?

NOTE Contractions are usually used in spoken English.

The present tense (**base/base + -s**) is used to describe generalizations based on (1) habits, (2) routines, and (3) facts:

1. Habits are things you do regularly:

   I **shake** hands whenever I **meet** someone new.

2. Routines are things you do every day:

   My roommate **gets** up at 7:30 and **makes** coffee.

3. Facts are always true (or else they are no longer facts):

   Approximately three-quarters of the U.S. labor force **is** white, non-Hispanic.

PRACTICE

Activity 1

Partners. Refer to your responses to statements about job interview behavior in the the list in the Preview. Compare your answers with those of a partner. Underline the number corresponding to your partner's responses to the statements.

Activity 2

Groups or whole class. Report your findings about your partner's responses in Activity 1 orally or in writing.

1. If you report orally, ask another student to listen to what you say. Did you use the **-s** ending on the verbs?
2. If you report in writing, ask another student to read your report. Did you use the **-s** ending on the verbs?

Activity 3

Three of the 13 statements listed on page 7 are *not* job interview tips recommended by the U.S. Bureau of Labor Statistics. In your opinion, which of the statements are not recommended? See the end of this lesson for the answer.

BE (am/are/is) + -ing (present progressive). The expanded verb **BE + -ing** (present progressive) has two parts: the **auxiliary verb,** which is a form of BE, and the **-ing** form of another verb. In the present, BE takes the form **am/are/is,** as in Table 1.3.

TABLE 1.3 Forming **BE (am/are/is) + -ing** (present progressive)

STATEMENT			NEGATIVE			QUESTION		
I	am	working.	I	am I'm	not working.	Am	I	working?
You We They	are	working.	You We They	are not aren't	working.	Are	you we they	working?
She He It	is	working.	She He It	is not isn't	working.	Is	she he it	working?

BE + -ing describes an action that

1. begins or takes place now (in the present) and often continues into the future:
   - I'm filling out an application form for a job.
   - My sister Kristina is working at the Community Center this summer.
2. is temporary, not permanent:
   - She's not earning a lot of money this summer. (a one-time event in the future -> **BE + -ing**)
   - She works for the city's recreation programs every summer. (a habitual event -> **simple present**)
3. happens in the near future:
   - Kristina is leaving for college in the fall.
   - She's buying a car at the end of August.
4. The form **BE GOING to + Verb** is often used to describe actions in the future, especially in informal speech or writing:
   She's going to buy a used car.

BE + -ing is used with **active verbs,** verbs that describe an action or event. **BE + -ing** is normally not used with **stative verbs,** verbs that describe a mental or physical state or verbs of perception. Table 1.4 lists some common stative verbs.

TABLE 1.4 Common Stative Verbs

EMOTION	COGNITION	POSSESSION	PERCEPTION
appreciate	believe	belong	feel
hate	know	have	hear
like (dislike)	think	own	see
love	understand		smell
prefer			taste
want			touch

1. Correct:
   - Kristina likes to ride her bike to work.
   - Other people don't understand this.
2. Incorrect:
   - She is wanting to buy a car before the fall.

For more information about **BE + -ing,** see *The Tapestry Grammar,* Chapter 8, pages 186–188 and 206–208.

Activity 4

Complete the following sentences, using the appropriate form of the **present tense** or **BE + -ing** (present progressive). In a few sentences, both are possible.

1. The Job Corps, a federally funded program, ________________ (provide) 62,000 young people a year with job skills training, high school and college coursework, and free housing.

2. A high school diploma ________________ (help) but ________________ (not guarantee) a job in today's market.

3. In the course of their careers, college graduates ________________ (earn) 77 percent more than those without degrees.

4. But as high school graduates, many young people like Kristina only ________________ (earn) the minimum wage in the summer.

5. As they move into the global marketplace, companies ________________ (look) for people who can adapt to other cultures.

6. That's one reason why Kristina ________________ (go) to take a course in Japanese this fall in college.

7. To be successful, a person ________________ (need) advanced training, but not necessarily at a four-year college.

8. For example, Rachelle Brown, 19, ________________ (train) to become a solar installer at the San Diego Job Corps.

9. She ________________ (want) to be in a field with a future, and in the San Diego area, solar installation ________________ (be) in demand.

10. Lans Pursel, 21, ________________ (not have) a high school diploma.

11. Now Pursel ________________ (get) training in the San Diego Job Corps.

12. He ________________ (prepare) for jobs in building maintenance, plumbing, electrical work or solar installation.

Activity 5

Practice with question formation. To compare labor statistics in the United States and Canada, you needed to get some information about Canada, so you called the Reference Center of Statistics Canada in Ottawa, Ontario (Tel: 800 267-6677). You received the following answers to your questions. Write an appropriate question for each of the answers. The first one is done for you. Before you begin, you may want to review question formation in *The Tapestry Grammar,* Chapter 2, pages 13-20.

1. YOU: *What is the population of Canada today?*

   STATISTICS CANADA (SC): The total population of Canada is about 27,600,000. In the 1991 Census, it was about 27,300,000.

2. YOU: ________________________________

   SC: There are nearly 14 million Canadians in the labor force.

3. YOU: ________________________________

   SC: The labor force includes all Canadians aged 15 years and older.

4. YOU: ________________________________

   SC: No, Canada doesn't divide up labor force statistics into major ethnic groups anymore.

5. YOU: ________________________________

   SC: The median wage for Canadian workers was $19,438 in 1992. But remember, that's Canadian dollars.

6. YOU: ________________________________

   SC: About 51 percent of the labor force is female.

7. YOU ________________________________

   SC: The median income of women was $14,534 in 1992. That's about 57 percent of the median income for men in the same year, or $25,580.

8. YOU ________________________________

   SC: Yes, the gap in income between men and women is closing.

Adapted from Statistics Canada

LEARNING STRATEGY

Managing Your Learning: Paying attention to your ideas first and then editing for grammar, spelling, and punctuation will help you focus on content before grammar when you write.

Activity 6

In a paragraph, describe your ideal job using the present tense and **BE + -ing.** Include the responsibilities your job requires, any other requirements for the job, the time schedule, and the pay or salary.

Answer to Activity 3: Statements 6, 7, and 11.

Lesson 3: Verb Endings

Simple Past -ed, BE (was/were) + -ing

PREVIEW

Ask yourself or a partner:

1. Where were you in the summer of 1993?
2. What were you doing? Were you working? Were you taking it easy?
3. Did you hear about the floods in the Midwestern states in the United States?

Read the passage and then answer the questions that follow.

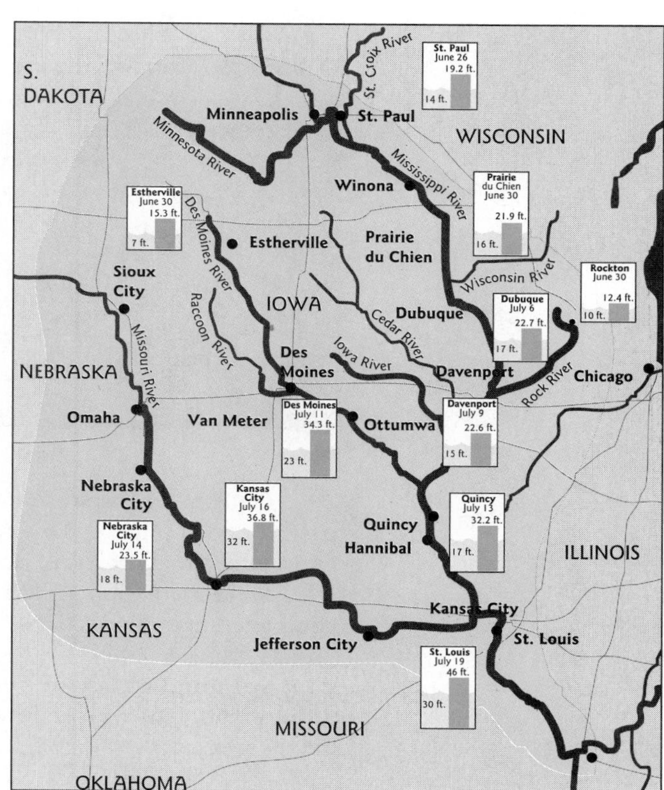

Map of flood areas in the Midwest, Summer 1993.

THE FLOOD OF SUMMER 1993

(1) From Minneapolis/St. Paul, Minnesota, to St. Louis, Missouri, the summer of 1993 was one to remember. (2) Not only was it the wettest summer in nearly 100 years, but heavy rains resulted in **record** floods in a number of states, including Wisconsin, Iowa, Illinois, and Missouri. (3) The most damage occurred in towns and cities along the Mississippi River and its **tributaries.** (4) North to south in **domino-like** fashion, **levees** broke, fields flooded, **sewers** backed up, businesses and homes were damaged or destroyed, and lives were **uprooted.** (5) Because of the urgent needs in many communities, people of all types were working side by side. (6) As they worked, they were learning something about human nature as well as Mother Nature.

record (adj.) highest point
tributary a smaller river that flows into a larger river
domino-like like a chain reaction, when one thing affects others one after the next
levee a manmade wall constructed to protect against high water
sewer underground pipes for carrying liquid and solid waste with rain water
uproot pull up, completely disrupt

1. Circle the simple **past tense verbs** in the reading. Some sentences may have more than one past tense verb. (See the next section, Presentation, if you're not sure which verbs are past tense.)

   NOTE Be careful with the verbs in sentence 4. Expanded verbs with the form **BE + -ed** are in the passive voice (Lesson 4), not the simple past tense.

2. Underline the expanded verbs with the form **BE (was/were) + -ing** (past progressive) in the passage.
3. How many *different* simple past tense verbs did you find?

   ____

4. How many *different* BE + -ing **verbs did you find?**

   ____

PRESENTATION

Simple past. **Regular verbs** in the past tense end with **-ed.** If the **base** of a regular verb ends in **-e,** then only **-d** is added to form the past tense (hire → hire**d**, manage → manage**d**). Table 1.5 gives examples of how to form the past tense.

TABLE 1.5 Forming the Past Tense (**base + -ed**)

STATEMENT		NEGATIVE			QUESTION		
I You We They	helped.	I You We They	did not didn't	help.	Did	I you we they	help?
She He It	helped.	She He It	did not didn't	help	Did	she he it	help?

English speakers use the past tense to refer to events or actions completed in the past. It doesn't matter how recently or how long ago an action was completed. What is important is that the event occurred and was completed at a definite time in the past.

Time markers, such as "ago," "yesterday," and "in 1990," are often used to mark completed events or actions in the past.

Spelling: Irregular verbs in the past. **Irregular verbs** change from their base forms in different ways to form the past tense. Table 1.6 lists five types of spelling changes that may occur.

LEARNING STRATEGY

Remembering New Material: Grouping similar verb forms together can help you remember irregular past tense verbs.

TABLE 1.6 Spelling Changes with Irregular Past Tense Verbs

TYPE OF CHANGE	EXAMPLES	
	Base	**Past**
Vowel change	eat get write	**ate** **got** **wrote**
Consonant change	send make build	sen**t** ma**d**e buil**t**
Consonant + vowel change	do feel sleep	**did** **felt** **slept**
Complete change	be go	**was/were** **went**
No change	cost put set	cost put set

For more information about the simple past tense, see *The Tapestry Grammar,* Chapter 8, pages 180–183. Also see the list of Common Irregular Verbs at the end of *The Tapestry Grammar*.

Pronunciation: Regular verbs in the simple past. The **-ed** ending *looks* the same in regular past tense verbs, but, depending on the verb, **-ed** is pronounced as [d], [t] or [ɪd] (an extra syllable).* The **-ed** is pronounced as [ɪd], with an extra syllable, only in regular verbs that end in a [d] or a [t] sound (e.g., fol<u>d</u>, prin<u>t</u>). There are also rules for predicting when to pronounce the other **-ed** sounds, but knowing when to add the extra syllable [ɪd] is the most important pronunciation rule. See *The Tapestry Grammar,* Chapter 8, pages 180–181, for more information on pronunciation of **-ed.**

*The brackets [ ] indicate the pronunciation, not the spelling, of a word or sound.

PRACTICE

Activity 1

Read the following past tense verbs from the passage "The Flood of Summer 1993" aloud and listen to how you (or a native speaker of English) pronounce **-ed**: *occurred, learned, backed, worked, resulted, flooded.* Did you hear the three pronunciations of **-ed**? Table 1.7 lists these verbs according to their pronunciation of **-ed.**

TABLE 1.7 Pronunciation of Past Tense (**base + -ed**)

[d]	[t]	[ɪd]*
occurr**ed**	back**ed**	result**ed**
learn**ed**	work**ed**	flood**ed**

*Pronounced with an extra syllable. For example, **re-sult** = two syllables; **re-sult-ed** = three syllables.

Activity 2

Alone or with a partner, read the following verbs and listen carefully to how you pronounce **-ed**: *rained, helped, wanted, added, missed, destroyed, damaged, saved.* Then write how **-ed** is pronounced ([d], [t], or [ɪd]). Check your work with your teacher or a native speaker of English. The first one is done for you.

VERB	PRONUNCIATION OF -ED
rained	[d]
helped	______
wanted	______
added	______
missed	______
destroyed	______
damaged	______
saved	______

BE (was/were) + -ing (past progressive). The expanded verb **BE + -ing** (past progressive) has two parts: the **auxiliary verb,** which is a form of BE **(was/were),** and the **-ing** form of another verb. Table 1.8 summarizes the formation of the past progressive.

TABLE 1.8 Forming **was/were + -ing** (past progressive)

STATEMENT			NEGATIVE			QUESTION		
I	was	eating.	I	was not / wasn't	eating.	Was	I	eating?
You / We / They	were	eating.	You / We / They	were not / weren't	eating.	Were	you / we / they	eating?
She / He / It	was	eating.	She / He / It	was not / wasn't	eating.	Was	she / he / it	eating?

Was/were + -ing is often used to indicate

1. an ongoing action in the past:
   - What **were** you **doing** in the summer of 1993?
   - I **was working** part-time.
2. an ongoing action in the past that is interrupted by a completed action:
   - I **was watching** TV when the electricity went off.
   - I **was searching** frantically for my radio until my roommate accidentally bumped into it.
   - While I **was listening** to the radio, a flood warning was announced.
3. an ongoing action that occurs along with another ongoing action:
   - The rain **was pouring** down while I **was listening** to the radio.
   - I **was rushing** around the house and **packing** some food and clothes to bring with me.

Words used to indicate time clauses, such as <u>when</u> and <u>while</u>, are commonly used to describe ongoing events or completed events in the past. <u>Until</u> introduces a time clause describing a completed event as sentence 2 shows.

For more information on **BE (was/were) + -ing,** see *The Tapestry Grammar,* Chapter 8, pages 206–207.

LEARNING STRATEGY

Forming Concepts: Paying attention to time markers helps you decide which verb tense to use.

Activity 3

Fill in the appropriate verb form in the blanks below with the **present tense, the past tense,** or **was/were + -ing.** In some sentences, either the **past tense** or **was/were + -ing** is possible.

FLOOD BONDS FARMERS WITH FELONS

HILLVIEW, ILL. July 27—(1) This ________________ (be) a story of black and Hispanic drug dealers from Chicago who tried to help white farmers and factory workers save their town. (2) They ________________ (work) side by side from July 2 to July 10 and ________________ (lose) their fight against the river, but in the fight, they ________________ (find) each other. (3) The town, under water since July 10, 1993, ________________ (be) Niota, Illinois. (4) The dealers, who belong to a **boot camp prison program** in Greene County, have moved downriver, throwing sandbags in Quincy, Hardin, Marblehead, and this week, in Hillview. (5) But they still ________________ (talk) of Niota—the people in Niota, the food they ________________ (eat) in Niota, the songs they ________________ (sing) in Niota—like it ________________ (be) home. (6) Today the **inmates** ________________ (**choke up**) over a card that had arrived at the boot camp **barracks.** (7) There ________________ (be) a picture of roses and a message: "With warmest thanks to each of you, from your Niota family. You'll never be forgotten."

Slightly adapted from S. Rimer, "Flood Bonds Farmers with Felons, Transforming Them All," *The New York Times,* July 29, 1993.

felon a person convicted of a serious crime, such as drug dealing, murder, or burglary
boot camp prison program a military-style work program for individuals convicted of serious but nonviolent crimes
inmates prisoners who live in the same prison or residence
choke up become visibly emotional about something
barracks military-style housing for prisoners or soldiers

Activity 4

Read the excerpt about the boot camp inmates' struggle against the flooding in Niota, Illinois. Use the **simple past** or **was/were + -ing,** as appropriate. In some cases, either the **simple past** or **was/were + -ing** can be used.

(1) Thirty residents of Niota ______________ (sign) the card to the boot camp inmates who had tried to save their town. (2) One ______________ (be) Neoma Farr, the "orange drink lady." (3) "They ______________ (be) crazy about that orange drink. (4) It ______________ (be) so hot. (5) We ______________ (have) to make sure they ______________ (have) plenty to drink. (6) I couldn't get over how hard they ______________ (work). (7) And they ______________ (thank) me for every **itty bitty thing.**"

(8) Greg Lance, 23, ______________ (be) 10 years old when his father was **fatally** shot at his housing project in Chicago. (9) A few years later, he ______________ (join) the Vice Lords gang. (10) But he ______________ (cry) the day the levee ______________ (break) in Niota. (11) "A lot of people ______________ (lose) their homes. (12) They ______________ (be) always ______________ (thank) us. (13) Thank us for what? (14) We were confused. (15) It ______________ (not help). (16) Maybe we should've worked harder, or faster.

(17) The superintendent of the boot camp, John W. McCorkle, is a 6-foot 5-inch Vietnam **veteran** who dresses in black, rarely takes off his sunglasses, and shouts at inmates when they forget to call him "sir." (18) But he ______________ (cry) openly over the levee. (19) "I always ______________ (know) boot camp kids work hard. (20) But they ______________ (amaze) me. (21) They ______________ (throw) sandbags and ______________ (smile), and I ______________ (ask) them, 'What are you smiling for?' (22) They ______________ (answer) back, 'We're saving lives, sir!'"

itty bitty thing everything, large and small
fatally causing death
veteran someone who has been an active member of the armed forces

Activity 5

Read the following paragraph about a very different type of work and then complete the activity.

Ben Cohen, left, and Jerry Greenfield sample their wares.

ICE CREAM DIPLOMACY

(1) Meet Ben Cohen and Jerry Greenfield. (2) They opened their first **scoop shop** in Burlington, Vermont, in 1978. (3) Today, they have scoop shops in 18 states in the United States and four other countries. (4) A new scoop shop and ice cream factory recently opened in Petrozavodsk, Karelia, a former northern Soviet Republic near Finland.

diplomacy the art or practice of conducting international relations, for example, negotiating treaties and agreements
scoop shop a shop where ice cream is sold and served

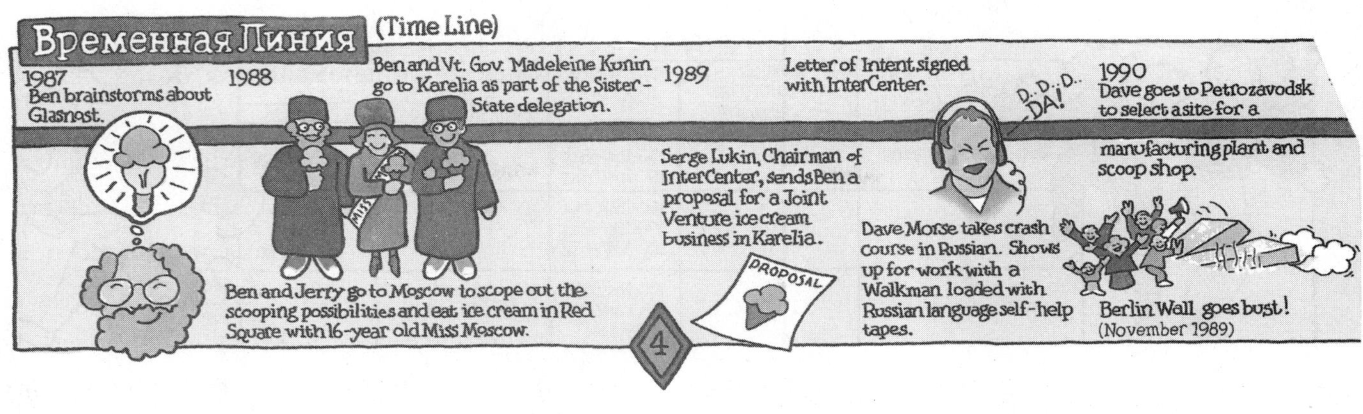

Source: Ben & Jerry's Chunk Mail, Vol. 1 (2), 1992. Reprinted by permission.

1. Read the timeline of events leading to the opening of Ben & Jerry's in Karelia. Discuss any vocabulary that is new.
2. Then rewrite the events in the timeline using the past tense. The first one is done for you.

a. 1987—*In 1987 Ben brainstormed about glasnost.*

b. 1988—____________________

c. 1988—____________________

d. 1989—____________________

e. 1989—____________________

f. 1989—____________________

g. 1990—____________________

h. 1990—____________________

i. 1990—____________________

j. 1990—____________________

k. 1991—____________________

l. 1991—____________________

m. 1992—____________________

n. 1992—____________________

o. 1992—____________________

Activity 6

Here is a more complete version of how Ben & Jerry's scoop shop and ice cream factory in Karelia started. Fill in the blanks with the **simple past** or **was/were + -ing,** as appropriate. In a few sentences, both are possible.

(1) After a **joint venture** agreement was signed by the two parties in September 1990, Ben & Jerry's Vermont-Karelia Ice Cream, or Iceverks, ________________ (be) a reality . . . on paper, that is. (2) Then Dave Morse, an experienced production supervisor, ________________ (enter) the scene. (3) He ________________ (become) the American co-manager of the joint venture and eagerly ________________ (agree) not only to be Ben & Jerry's main man in Karelia but also to take a **crash course** in basic Russian.

(4) By the beginning of 1991, Dave and his family had taken up residence in Karelia and ________________ (begin) the task of making Iceverks a reality. (5) Getting the ice cream factory **infrastructure** in place ________________ (be) a lengthy and often frustrating process in a country full of changes. (6) Dave, his family, and the Iceverks crew ________________ (have) to deal with materials **shortages,** language barriers, confusing bureaucratic processes, and unethical construction contractors. (7) In the middle of it all, in August 1991, the attempted **overthrow** of Gorbachev's government ________________ (occur). (8) After several tense weeks and many examples of heroic resistance from the Russian people, life ________________ gradually ________________ (return) to "normal" and the renovation of the sports and cultural events center into a scoop shop/ice cream factory ________________ (continue).

(9) In early 1992 huge containers of materials needed for setting up the factory and scoop shop in Karelia were packed and shipped to Petrozavodsk. (10) Finally, in July 1992, Iceverks ________________ (open), with the blessing of a Russian Orthodox priest. (11) Ben & Jerry's and InterCenter had succeeded in bridging cultural differences and establishing a joint venture. (12) As one satisfied Russian customer ________________ (put) it, "It doesn't matter if the place is Russian or American, as long as the ice cream is good."

Based on "Ice Cream Diplomacy," *Ben and Jerry's Chunk Mail.*

joint venture a business partnership between two companies or countries
crash course a short, intensive course
infrastructure the basic facilities and equipment needed to establish a business
shortage an insufficient amount
overthrow downfall of something, often by force

Activity 7

Combine the following phrases into sentences. Use the time markers in some items to guide your choice of verb tense (simple present, BE + -ing, simple past. When you are done, you will have a paragraph about Bob Humke, a man who works for recreation. Rembember to add a period at the end of each sentence and a comma after some of the phrases, as needed.

1. The son of a high school basketball coach/ Bob Humke grow up playing sports and enjoying games
2. When Humke be 22 years old/ he decide to pursue a career in recreation
3. Humke serve a four-year hitch in the Navy/ when he read a magazine article about a recreation director in New Jersey who help poor children

4. Humke return to Wisconsin/ and get a bachelor's degree in physical education and recreation at UW-La Crosse in 1963
5. After working for the recreation department in several cities/ Humke earn a master's degree in recreation at Indiana University in 1967
6. In 1980/ Humke become director of Madison School-Community Recreation (MSCR)/ which run recreation programs for 40,000 children and adults in Madison
7. As director/ Humke oversee 21 full-time employees and more than 1,500 part-time and seasonal employees
8. Besides running large basketball and softball leagues/ MSCR offer recreation programs in swimming, tennis, canoeing, and even ballroom dancing
9. He receive $74,470 a year for his work
10. Humke want MSCR to focus more on improving the lives of poor children through recreation in the future

Based on Joel Broadway, "MSCR Director Makes Fun His Game,"
Wisconsin State Journal, June 25, 1995.

Lesson 4: BE + -d/t/n (Passive Voice)

PREVIEW

Some people don't leave home without their favorite brand of shampoo, toothpaste, or hand lotion in their luggage.

Ask yourself or a partner:

1. Do you use any skin and hair care products regularly? If you do, list them by brand name.

   ____

   ____

2. Are any natural ingredients used to make them? If you know any natural ingredients in the products you use, list them below:

   ____

Read the passage and answer the questions that follow.

THE BODY SHOP

In March 1976, Anita Roddick, an ex-schoolteacher, opened a small shop in Brighton on England's south coast. She sold 25 naturally-based skin and hair products. These products were bottled in five sizes so that customers could buy as much or as little as they wanted. Mrs. Roddick started her business because she needed to make money to support her two daughters and herself while her husband Gordon was fulfilling his lifelong dream: traveling by horseback from Buenos Aires to New York. Mr. Roddick didn't make it to New York, but his wife's business **took off.**

In 18 years, Mrs. Roddick turned her small **cosmetics** store in England into The Body Shop, a worldwide chain with over 1,000 shops trading in 45 countries and in 19 languages. Today she and her husband run the company, which earned a $34 million profit in 1993. At The Body Shop, no animals are used to test products, bottles are refilled or recycled for customers who choose to bring them back, and many of the ingredients are gathered from natural sources. Employees are encouraged to participate in company-supported political programs, like the 1992 voter registration drive in the USA and the signing of an international agreement to protect the environment in 1993.

Adapted from the newsletter, *This Is The Body Shop,* Spring 1994, and Trish Hall, "Striving to Be Cosmetically Correct," *New York Times,* May 27, 1993.

take off start to become successful
cosmetics products, such as skin cream and lipstick, designed to beautify the body

In the above passage, the underlined verbs are **passive** in form and meaning. Unlike subjects in sentences with active verbs, subjects in each of these sentences are *not* the "doers" of the actions described. Compare the two sentences below:

- Employees encourage others to participate in company-supported political programs.
- Employees are encouraged to participate in company-supported political programs.

1. Who is responsible for the action in the first sentence above?

____

In the second sentence?

____

2. Which sentence, the first or the second, contains a passive verb?

____

PRESENTATION

A **passive verb** always has at least two parts: the auxiliary verb, which contains a form of BE, and the **-d/t/n** form (past participle) of another verb. **Basic passive verbs** use the simple present or simple past forms of BE + the -d/t/n form of another verb:

	BE	-d/t/n form	
No animals	{ **are** / **were** }	**used**	to test products.

Table 1.9 shows how to form the basic passive.

TABLE 1.9 Forming Basic Passive Verbs (**BE + -d/t/n**)

FORM OF BE	STATEMENT	QUESTION
Simple present	The bottle { is / isn't } refilled.	Is the bottle refilled?
	The bottles { are / aren't } refilled.	Are the bottles refilled?
Simple past	The bottle { was / wasn't } refilled.	Was the bottle refilled?
	The bottles { were / weren't } refilled.	Were the bottles refilled?

The **-d/t/n** form of the verb varies from the **base** form in various ways. Table 1.10 divides these changes into three verb "families."

TABLE 1.10 Verb Families

VERB FAMILY	BASE FORM	BASE + -ed (past tense)	-d/t/n FORM
All forms different	get	got	gotten
	sing	sang	sung
Two forms the same			
Regular verbs	manage	managed	managed
	work	worked	worked
Irregular verbs	keep	kept	kept
	tell	told	told
All forms the same	let	let	let
	put	put	put

Passive verbs are used for three general reasons:

1. to avoid using the same subject in a series of sentences
2. to avoid saying who or what is responsible for the actions that are described
3. to put the noun phrase that describes who or what is responsible for the action toward the end of the sentence (instead of in the subject position at the beginning).

However, using the passive too often is not considered good style. So use the passive when you want to keep the topic the same in a series of sentences or when some information is not important or not known. For further information on **passive verbs,** see *The Tapestry Grammar,* Chapter 9, pages 226--235, and the list of Common Irregular Verbs at the end of *The Tapestry Grammar*.

LEARNING STRATEGY

Remembering New Material: Grouping similar verb forms together in verb families can help you remember them.

PRACTICE

Activity 1

Read some beliefs about how Anita and Gordon Roddick run The Body Shop. Change the statements about their beliefs so that the emphasis is on how The Body Shop operates instead of on the Roddicks. The first one is done for you.

The Body Shop believes in an honest approach to selling cosmetics:

1. They recycle containers when customers bring them back.
   Containers are recycled when customers bring them back.
   ____
2. They don't promote images of perfect women.
   ____
3. They design their products to meet the real needs of people, so they sell all their products in multiple sizes.
   ____
   ____
4. They don't test their products or ingredients on animals.
   ____
5. They refill containers on demand.
   ____
6. They use minimal packaging.
   ____

Activity 2

Complete the following descriptions of Body Shop products from different parts of the world. Use the appropriate form of the passive verb.

BRAZIL. The Body Shop has developed links with the Kayapo Indians in the eastern Amazon basin. The Kayapo produce Brazil nut oil from nuts they harvest from the rain forest. The nuts ______(1)______ (use) to make Brazil Nut Oil Conditioner. They also make beaded wristbands for sales in some branches of The Body Shop. Money from the project ______(2)______ (pay) into a community fund, which ______(3)______ (administer) by tribal chiefs. It ______(4)______ (use) to pay for community needs, such as an airplane to transport villagers who need medical attention.

TANZANIA/ZAMBIA. Organic honey and beeswax ______(5)______ (use) for Honey Stick, a pocket-sized lip balm that protects against the sun and wind. The organic honey comes from honey-making cooperatives in these two countries. The cooperatives ______(6)______ (make) up of forest communities who harvest the honey from the traditional bark beehives. These beehives ______(7)______ (hang) throughout the forest.

NEW MEXICO, USA. Blue corn ______(8)______ (grow) and ______(9)______ (process) by the Santa Ana Pueblo Indians. It is the basis for products such as Blue Corn Scrub Masks. Blue corn oil, another skin care product, ______(11)______ (derive) from Indian corn in the Southwest.

Based on *This Is The Body Shop* newsletter (Spring 1994).

Activity 3

Passive verbs are often found in textbooks and in descriptions of scientific or technical processes. Complete the following description about glassmaking with recycled glass, using the appropriate form of the **simple present** or the **basic passive verb.** In the passage that follows, **expanded passive verbs,** which contain two or more auxiliaries, are underlined.

BACKGROUND. People have been making glass for approximately 3,500 years. Most glass ______(1)______ (made) of three basic ingredients: white sand, soda, and lime. The materials ______(2)______ (heat) to around 2,500°F, until they ______(3)______ completely ______(4)______ (dissolve) and transparent. Then the mixture ______(5)______ (cool) to around 1,800°F. The whole process ______(6)______ (take) about 7,600 BTUs* of energy to produce a single pound of glass.

Before recycled glass ______(7)______ (ship) to the manufacturers, it ______(8)______ (break) so it will take up less volume. This broken glass ______(9)______ (call) *cullet.* When it ______(10)______ (arrive) at the factory, cullet ______(11)______ (run) through a magnetic device designed to remove plastic rings from bottles. A vacuum process ______(12)______

* BTU (British thermal unit) = the amount of heat required to raise the temperature of one pound of water by 1°F.

(remove) plastic coatings and paper labels; then the cullet ______ 13 (be) ready to be added into the mixture. Because cullet ______ 14 (lower) the melting temperature of the mixture in manufacturing glass, up to 32 percent less energy ______ 15 (require).

GLASS FACT: All glass bottles and jars can be recyled. But other types of glass, such as window panes, Pyrex, and light bulbs, ______ 16 (make) by different processes and can't be combined with the cullet to make glass containers.

From the Earthworks Group, *50 Simple Things You Can Do to Save the Earth.* Berkeley, CA: Earthworks Press, 1989.

Activity 4

Change in the classroom is sometimes related to better learning by students. Complete the following report, using the **simple past** or the **basic passive verb** in the past.

For years, Sandy Fitch ______ 1 (teach) business education at Yarmouth High School in Maine using textbooks and standardized tests. For years, she also ______ 2 (feel) there ______ 3 (have) to be another way. Sandy admits that even she ______ 4 (bore) by her old teaching methods. More important, she ______ 5 (concern) that her students weren't getting the hands-on training they would need to compete in the workplace.

So, in the spring of 1992, Sandy ______ 6 (decide) to try a different approach: Macintosh personal computers. She ______ 7 (develop) a three-month-long project in which each student ______ 8 (ask) to complete 11 business-related activities—all on the computer. They (write) resumes. They ______ 9 (assemble) data bases of employees ______ 10 and salaries. They ______ 11 (produce) a company newsletter. They even ______ 12 (create) a corporate profit/loss statement. After they ______ 13 (do) this, the students ______ 14 (evaluate) on their innovation and creativity and on their ability to follow directions and write. "What a difference!" Sandy says. "Their work—and their evaluations—______ 15 (improve) dramatically."

Adapted from an Apple Computer, Inc., advertisement in *Discover,* June 1994, Vol. 15 (6), page 69.

Activity 5

Partners or Groups. Why did the students improve their work in the business education class at Yarmouth High School? Do you think their improvement was caused by the use of computers, the use of a new teaching method, the teacher's renewed interest in the course, or something else? Discuss your ideas and summarize them in about a page. After writing, review your summary for the appropriate use of the passive with your partner or the group.

Lesson 5: HAVE (have/has) + -d/t/n (Present Perfect)

PREVIEW

WHO IS SHE ? ? ?

Read the background information about this well-known U.S. comedienne and actress and then try to guess who she is.

- She grew up in New York City.
- She began acting when she was eight.
- She has worked professionally as a comedienne since 1979.
- In her first film, she played Celie, the heroine of *The Color Purple* (1985), directed by Steven Spielberg.
- She won an Oscar for best supporting actress as a fake ghost in the popular movie *Ghost* (1985).
- Film critics have described her as a liberated Hattie McDaniel, who played Mammy in *Gone with the Wind* (1939).
- She has impressed *Star Trek* lovers as Guinan in *Star Trek: The Next Generation*.
- In 1994 she hosted the Oscar awards.

1. Who is she? ______________________________
   (See the end of the lesson for the answer.)
2. Three of the statements about this person use the **HAVE + -d/t/n** form (present perfect) instead of the past tense. Mark those sentences with a star (★).
3. Can you explain why **HAVE + -d/t/n** verb forms are used in these sentences?

   ____

   ____

PRESENTATION

HAVE (have/has) + -d/t/n (present perfect) is another example of an expanded verb. It combines a form of HAVE (have or has) with the **-d/t/n** form (the past participle). Table 1.11 gives examples of statements and questions with HAVE + -d/t/n.

TABLE 1.11 Forming **HAVE + -d/t/n** (present perfect)

STATEMENT	NEGATIVE	QUESTION
I / You / We / They { have / 've } worked.	I / You / We / They { have not / haven't } worked.	Have { I / you / we / they } worked?
She / He / It { has / 's } worked.	She / He / It { has not / hasn't } worked.	Has { she / he / it } worked?

Like past tense forms, the **-d/t/n** form can be regular or irregular. In regular verbs, the **-d/t/n** form is made by adding **-ed** or **-d** to the base. In irregular verbs, the **-d/t/n** form usually requires a change in the base form before ending in **-d, -t,** or **-n.** See Lesson 4 or *The Tapestry Grammar,* Chapter 9, pages 230–233, for more information about the three groups of **-d/t/n** forms.

LEARNING STRATEGY

Managing Your Learning: Writing the base form, past form, and -d/t/n form of a verb on cards and then grouping them into verb "families" can help you learn related verb forms.

Sentences with **have/has + -d/t/n** make a connection between past and present time in three ways:*

1. To describe events in the indefinite past that are relevant to the present (the emphasis is on the event, not on when it occurred):
   - **Has** this actress ever **won** an Oscar?
   - Yes, she **has**—for best supporting actress.
2. To describe habitual action or events in the past that are relevant to the present:
   - She **has acted** in several films since 1985.
   - In addition to films, she **has starred** in several one-woman productions of various funny or tragic characters.
3. To describe events or states that began in the past and continue up to the present:
   - She **has dreamed** of winning an Oscar since she was a child.
   - She **has lived** in California for more than 15 years.

*However, an event expressed in the present perfect may sometimes be expected to continue into the future; for example, *Marion Barry has lived in Washington, D.C. for years.*

Figure 1.2 sums up these three uses.

FIGURE 1.2 Three Uses of **HAVE + -d/t/n**

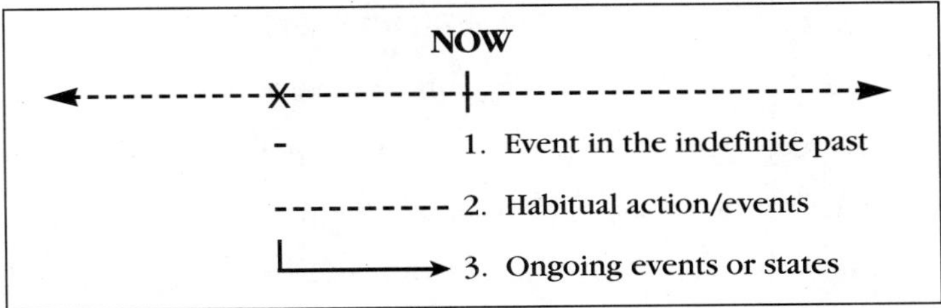

Choosing between **have/has + -d/t/n** and the **simple past** can sometimes be difficult. The following guidelines can help you decide between the two:*

1. Pay attention to time markers (in italic):
   - My boss has worked late several nights *this week.* (past-to-present time connection)
   - He also worked late several nights *last week.* (completed action in the past)
   - *Since* 1975, he has hired nearly 200 new workers. (the beginning point of an action/event that continues up to the present)
   - *For the past two decades,* wages and incomes in the United States have become more unequal. (the duration of past-to-present period)
   - *During* this period, wages and incomes have risen for upper-income workers, remained about the same for the middle class, and fallen for those at the bottom. (the duration of past-to-present period)

   Other common time markers used with HAVE + -d/t/n include "recently," "already," "just," "over the (years)," "yet" (in negative statements and questions).
2. Decide whether the past time includes the present or excludes the present:
   - She has worked in films since 1985. (past-to-present time = She has worked in films from 1985 to the present.)
   - She worked in New York for several years. (completed action in the past = She worked there until 1972.)
3. Consider the recency of events when there is no time marker (either HAVE + -d/t/n or the simple past may occur):
   - She has just completed a new movie. (emphasizes past-to-present time connection)
   - She just completed a new movie. (emphasizes completed action in the past)

   BUT NOT
   She has published a children's book, *Alice,* in 1992.
   (*In 1992* specifies a definite time in the past so that HAVE + -d/t/n is not appropriate here.)
4. Pay attention to past events with ties to the present (in boldface):
   - I haven't read *Alice,* so **I can't compare it to the book it is based on,** *Alice in Wonderland.*
5. Consider events in the indefinite past (With HAVE + -d/t/n, the fact that an event occurred at least once is important, not when it happened):
   - She's been to Paris, but she hasn't seen the Eiffel Tower. (she has never seen it)
   - She went to Paris, but she didn't see the Eiffel Tower. (she didn't see it during that trip, but perhaps she has seen it at another time)

*Based on Rodney Huddleston, *Introduction to the grammar of English,* Cambridge: Cambridge University Press, 1984.

For further information on HAVE + -d/t/n, see Chapter 8, pages 205–207, in *The Tapestry Grammar.*

PRACTICE

Activity 1

Individuals/Partners. Complete the following passage about women managers and the glass ceiling, an invisible barrier that prevents women from reaching the highest positions at work. Use **have/has + -d/t/n** (present perfect) or the **simple past** as appropriate. Then check your answers with a partner.

(1) American women are reaching for the top in many fields of work. (2) Perhaps the greatest advances ________________ (be) in the field of management. (3) However, women still ________________ (not gain) equality with men professionally or economically, according to the Women's Bureau of the U.S. Department of Labor. (4) Women managers who worked full-time in 1988 ________________ (earn) $23,356 on average. (5) Male managers' average earnings ________________ (be) $36,759 in

the same year. (5) Still, the income gap between men and women ________________ (narrow). (6) In 1979, women ________________ (make) 62.5 cents for every dollar males earned. Women now make 77 cents for every male dollar. (7) That's 1.5 cents better than in 1992.

(8) Although women executives have opened the board room doors, they ________________ (be) unable to reach the top posts of chairperson, vice-chairperson or president in many companies. (9) This phenomenon, known as *the glass ceiling,* represents the limits women can reach at the present time. (10) They can see through the glass ceiling but cannot move past it.

Adapted from "Women Managers on Increase in Many Jobs," *Beloit Daily News,* Oct. 28, 1992.

1. Have you ever experienced *the glass ceiling* or do you know someone who has experienced it?
2. What do you think women (and men) can do to break through or eliminate *the glass ceiling* on the job?

Activity 2

Read about Jay Leno, the comedian and host of *The Tonight Show*. Use the **past tense** or **HAVE + -d/t/n** as appropriate in the blanks. In some sentences, both are possible.

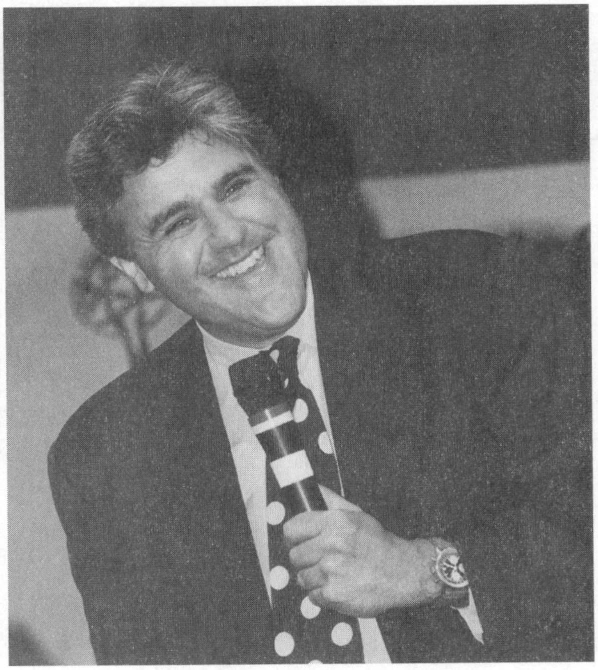

1. James Douglas Muir Leno ________________ (be born) 44 years ago in New Rochelle, New York, the grandson of Italian immigrants.
2. His family ______________ always ______________ (call) him "Jamie," but everyone else calls him "Jay."
3. Jay ________________ (begin) getting laughs for his lines when he was in the fourth grade.
4. He ________________ (graduate) from Emerson College in Boston in 1973, majoring in speech.
5. He ________________ (perform) his comedy act at night clubs in Boston, New York, and Los Angeles.
6. Jay first ________________ (appear) on *The Tonight Show* in 1977, with Johnny Carson as **host.**
7. Fifteen years later, Jay ________________ (replace) Carson as host, when Carson retired after nearly 30 years with the show.
8. Leno ________________ (host) *The Tonight Show* since May 1992.
9. Since August 1993, Jay's major competition on late night TV ________________ (be) David Letterman.
10. Somewhat ironically, when David Letterman hosted *The Tonight Show* in 1979, he once ______________ (invite) Jay to be a guest on the show.

Jay Leno

host a person who introduces a show and talks with guests on a TV or radio program

Activity 3

Individuals or groups. Interview someone at your school (not your English teacher) about his or her work experience. Use the following questions or ask questions of your own. Try to use HAVE + -d/t/n in some of your questions:

1. How long have you worked at your present job?
2. How did you get the job?
3. What do you like most about your job? What do you like least?
4. Have you ever worked in another country? If not, would you like to?
5. Have you ever wanted to do something else for a living?
6. ______________________________
7. ______________________________
8. ______________________________

Activity 4

Individuals or partners. Interview another person at your school or someone in your community who works in an area that interests you. Report your findings to your class or write up a short report on the person. Try to use HAVE + -d/t/n in some of your questions.

Activity 5

Practice with question formation. Refer to the charts from the U.S. Bureau of Labor Statistics, and then write questions for the answers that appear in boldface, using *how much, what* + noun, *when*, or *which* + noun. The first one is done for you. Before you begin, you may want to review question formation in *The Tapestry Grammar,* Chapter 2, pages 13–20.

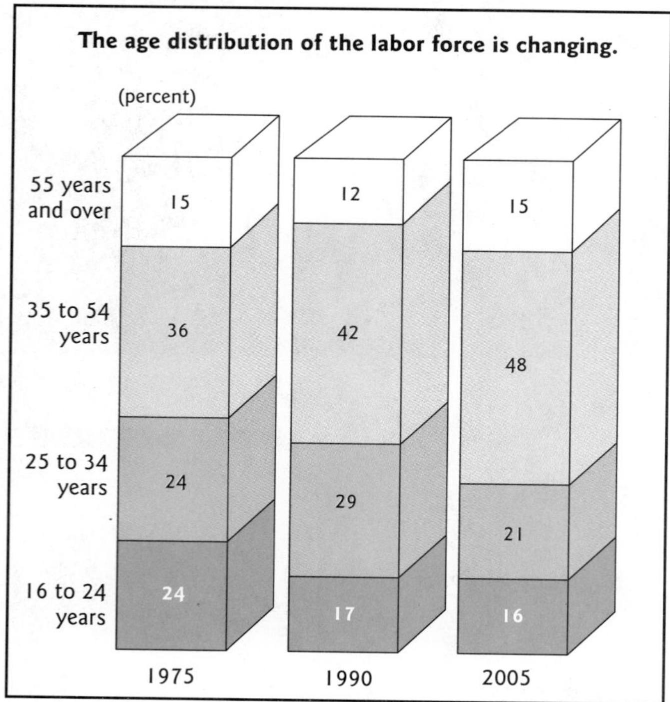

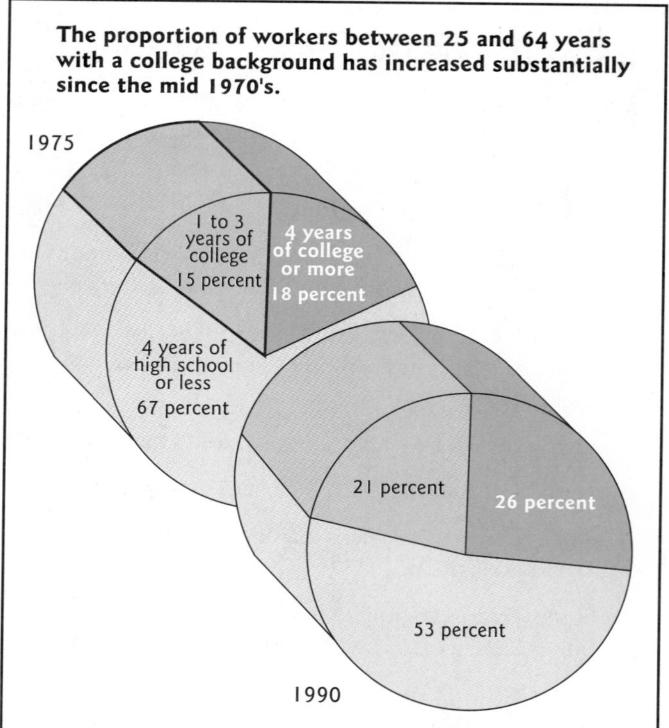

Source: U.S. Bureau of Labor Statistics, "Tomorrow's Jobs," in *Occupational Outlook Handbook.* Washington, DC: U.S. Department of Labor, 1992-93 edition.

1. *Which group of workers has increased the most since 1975?*

Since 1975, **workers 35 to 54 years old** have increased the most.

2. ______________________________

Since 1975, **workers 16 to 24 years old** have decreased the most.

3. ______________________________

Between 1975 and 2005, the proportion of workers 55 years and over is expected to remain about the same.

4. ______________________________

____

The proportion of workers with a college degree has grown **8 percentage points** since 1975.

5. ______________________________

____

The proportion of workers with four years of high school or less has shrunk **14 percentage points** since 1975.

6. ______________________________

____

The proportion of workers **with one to three years of college** has changed the least since the mid 1970s.

Your Opinion. Why do you think the proportion of workers with four years of high school or less has decreased over the years?

Activity 6.
***Which* + noun and *What* + noun in questions.**

1. Read the following questions:
   a. Which group of workers has increased the most since 1975?
   b. What group of workers has increased the most since 1975?
   Do you see any difference in meaning between the two questions?

   ____

Which + noun is generally used in questions with a *limited* number of possible answers (for example, one of four age groups in questions **a** and **b**). **What + noun** is used when there is an *unlimited* number of possible answers or when the number of possible answers is not known:

c. Which jobs are still available? (The choice is limited.)
d. What jobs require a college education? (The choice is unlimited or the number is not known.)

2. Write three pairs of questions with **which + noun** and **what + noun** about any topic. After the **which + noun** questions, explain how the choice of answers is limited.

Whoopi Goldberg is the person in the jumbled photo on page 24.

Lesson 6: Had + -d/t/n (Past Perfect)

PREVIEW

FOR YOUR INFORMATION The North American Trade Agreement (NAFTA) is an agreement between Canada, the United States, and Mexico. It was designed to encourage free trade between these countries, but some think it has resulted in the loss of jobs to countries where the cost of labor is less.

Source: Reprinted by permission: Tribune Media Services

Read the paragraph on NAFTA and then answer the questions.

In November 1993 the U.S. Congress approved the controversial North American Free Trade Agreement (NAFTA), which the Clinton Administration had carefully written and promoted as a way to save jobs. By that time, however, many U.S. industries and businesses, including big corporations like IBM and GM Motors, had already experienced serious downturns in profits as well as significant job losses.

1. Why do you think NAFTA was controversial at the time it was approved?
2. What is the job situation in your home country? Is the rate of unemployment increasing, decreasing, or staying the same?
3. If you are not working now, do you think it will be easy or difficult for you to get a job later?
4. There are two examples of **had + -d/t/n** (the past perfect) in the text. Find them and underline them.

PRESENTATION

As an expanded verb, **had + -d/t/n** (past perfect) combines the past form of HAVE (had) with the -d/t/n (past participle) form of the verb. Table 1.12 gives examples of statements and questions with had + -d/t/n.

TABLE 1.12 Forming **had + -d/t/n** (past perfect)

STATEMENT			NEGATIVE			QUESTION		
I You We They	{ had 'd }	gone.	I You We They	{ had not hadn't }	gone.	Had	{ I you we they }	gone?
She He It	} had	gone	She He It	{ had not hadn't }	gone.	Had	{ she he it }	gone?

Had + -d/t/n makes a connection between two events in the past when one event occurs before the other:

- In November 1993 the U.S. Congress **approved** NAFTA as a way to save jobs. (event 2, later event in the past)
- By that time, however, many U.S. industries and businesses **had already** experienced significant job losses. (event 1, earlier event in the past)

Had + -d/t/n is used with the earlier event, the loss of jobs (event 1). The **past tense** is used with the later event, the approval of NAFTA (event 2). Sometimes **had + -d/t/n** occurs alone in a sentence because the later event is understood:

- Some large companies **had** already **moved** factories out of the United States (later event [understood] = adoption of NAFTA)

Time markers with had + -d/t/n. Words and phrases, such as *by that time, after, before, when, until,* and *as soon as,* are often used with **had + -d/t/n.** These words and phrases mark time relationships between past time events.

- *As soon as* the students **had arrived** back on campus, parking spaces became hard to find.
- The first-year students could not register for courses *until* they **had seen** their academic advisors.

In informal usage, when time markers already indicate the order of two events in the past, the **past tense** may be used in the earlier time clause instead of **had + -d/t/n.**

- *After* classes **had started,** the students began to buy books.
  OR
- *After* classes **started,** the students began to buy books.

For further information on had + -d/t/n, see *The Tapestry Grammar,* Chapter 8, pages 204–207.

HAVE + -d/t/n makes a connection between the past and the present (present perfect) or between two events in the past (past perfect). **Had + -d/t/n** makes a connection between an earlier and a later event in the past. Figure 1.3 summarizes how HAVE and other auxiliaries show time relationships.

Figure 1.3 Time and Tense

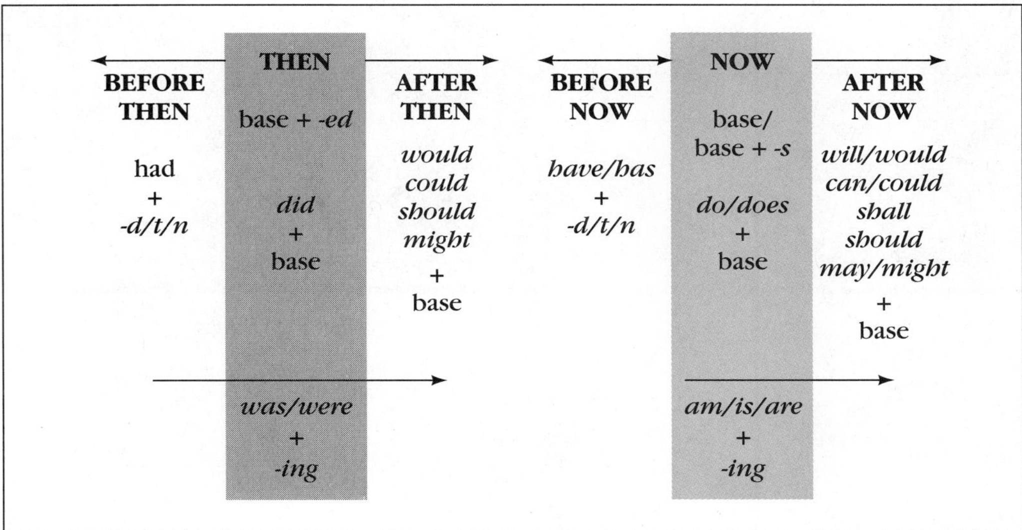

PRACTICE

Activity 1

Read about Garry Precision Screw Machine, a manufacturing company in New Jersey that would not die.

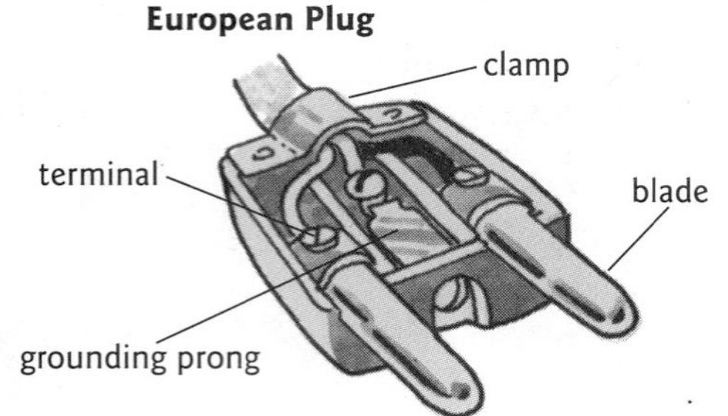

(1) Garry makes interconnect devices, the prongs and sockets that form the connections in electrical plugs. (2) All computers, microwave ovens, videocassette recorders and sophisticated weapons of war have thousands of tiny brass plugs, prongs, and soldering connections. (3) The founder of Garry, Mr. Koppell, built Garry into a $30 million-a-year business. (4) Like many other wealthy businessmen, he decided to sell his business and retire as a rich man. (5) The company passed from one international company to another. (6) In September 1992, the last owner, a $4 billion conglomerate, decided that it didn't need Garry's production any more and that the factory wasn't important enough to waste time looking for a buyer. (7) The owner simply shut down the company.

Based on Iver Peterson's article,
"Romantics of the Recession Fix Up Their Machine Shop."
The New York Times, July 20, 1993.

The sentences below use **had + -d/t/n** to relate two events in the past. Read them and then answer the questions. Notice the time markers (*in italics*) that occur with **had + -d/t/n**:

1. *By the time* Mr. Koppell sold the company, he **had built** it into a $30-million-a-year business.
2. Several international companies **had owned** and **sold** Garry *before* the $4-billion conglomerate bought it.
3. The most recent owner **had decided** the company wasn't important enough to look for a buyer *when* it shut down the factory.

WHAT ARE THE TWO EVENTS IN EACH OF THE SENTENCES 1–3?

	Event 1 (happened first)	Event 2 (happened second)
a.	________________	________________
b.	________________	________________
c.	________________	________________

When is **had + -d/t/n** used? ________________

____

When is the **past tense** used? ________________

____

Activity 2

Read what happened to the Garry plant after it shut down in September 1992. Fill in the blanks with the **past tense** or **had + -d/t/n** form, as appropriate. Use **had + -d/t/n** whenever possible.

(1) A few months after the Garry plant ________________ (close), Mr. Rueshoff and six other machinist **foremen** ________________ (enter) the factory to oil and turn the **bearings** on the precise cutting machines. (2) They ________________ (decide) to do this to prevent the bearings from drying out. (3) During this time, Sue Whitaker, who ________________ (work) in the main office, was sitting in her kitchen and calling suppliers of the materials the plant ________________ (use) in order to keep informed of prices. (4) She ________________ (give) the price information to Bob Lewis, who ________________ (be) the head of operations. (5) He ________________ (use) the information to **estimate** prices on jobs from a plant that technically ________________ (not exist) any more—and that he ________________ (not even work) for. (6) Mr. Mark, who ________________ (be) the plant manager, ________________ (begin) calling **former** customers and asking them if they ________________ (want) "to buy this place and put us all back to work." (7) After several calls, Wire-Pro Company in South Jersey ________________ (return) Mr. Mark's calls and ________________ (say) yes. (8) The auctioneer, who ________________ (be) in charge of selling the company's machinery to the highest **bidder,** also ________________ (agree). (9) To **sweeten the deal,** the New Jersey Commerce Department ________________ (offer) some financial **incentives** for Wire-Pro. (10) Finally, on July 12, 1993, Garry Precision Screw Machine Company ________________ (reopen) its doors. (11) A handful of dedicated workers ________________ (succeed) in saving the company.

Based on Iver Peterson, "Romantics of the Recession Fix Up Their Machine Shop." *New York Times,* July 20,1993.

foreman someone who is responsible for a group of workers in a manufacturing operation
bearing a small round part that reduces the friction between fixed and moving parts of a machine
estimate predict the expected cost
former previous; not current
bidder a person or a representative who makes an offer to buy something at an auction
sweeten the deal make a business agreement more attractive
incentive motivation to do something

Activity 3

Here is Angela's agenda during her first week of college classes in the fall. Write sentences that relate two past events using **had + -d/t/n.** Try to use some past perfect time markers (underlined). One is done for you as an example.

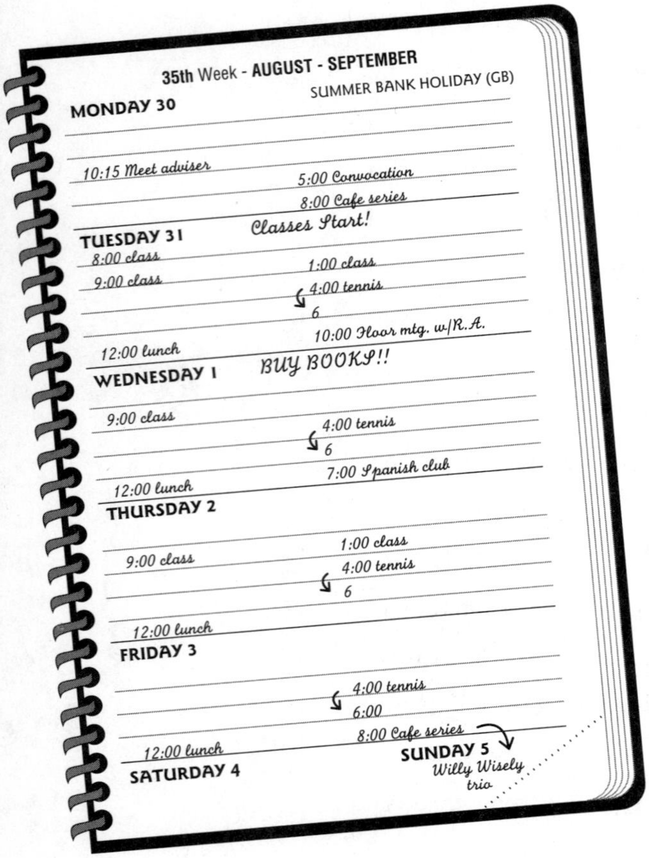

35th Week - AUGUST - SEPTEMBER

MONDAY 30 SUMMER BANK HOLIDAY (GB)
10:15 Meet adviser
5:00 Convocation
8:00 Cafe series

TUESDAY 31 Classes Start!
8:00 class
9:00 class
1:00 class
4:00 tennis
6
12:00 lunch
10:00 Floor mtg. w/R.A.

WEDNESDAY 1 BUY BOOKS!!
9:00 class
4:00 tennis
6
12:00 lunch
7:00 Spanish club

THURSDAY 2
9:00 class
1:00 class
4:00 tennis
6
12:00 lunch

FRIDAY 3
4:00 tennis
6:00
8:00 Cafe series
12:00 lunch

SATURDAY 4

SUNDAY 5 Willy Wisely trio

1. <u>When</u> classes began, Angela had <u>already</u> met with her advisor.
2. ______________________________
3. ______________________________
4. ______________________________
5. ______________________________
6. ______________________________
7. ______________________________
8. ______________________________

Activity 4

Partners.

Choice 1: Write a list of 10 things you have done in the past 24 hours along with the approximate time it took you to do them.

Choice 2: List the steps you take to write one of the following: science—a lab report; history—a brief biography; English—an essay; careers—a resume; your choice of writing.

Exchange lists with a partner, and then write four to five sentences about your partners' sentences using **had + -d/t/n** to relate two past events (as in Activity 3 with Angela's agenda). Try to use appropriate time markers with your sentences.

2 CHAPTER

Modals

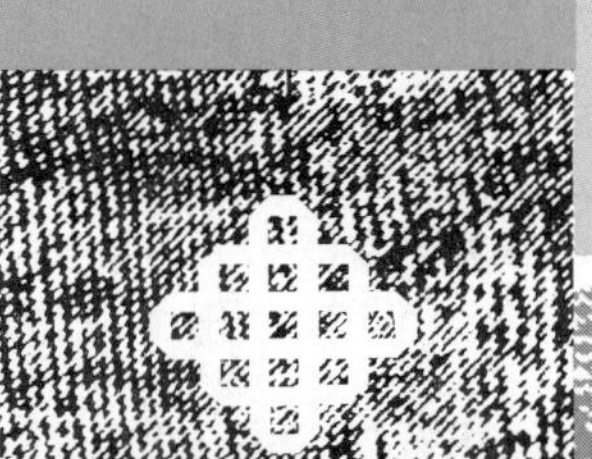

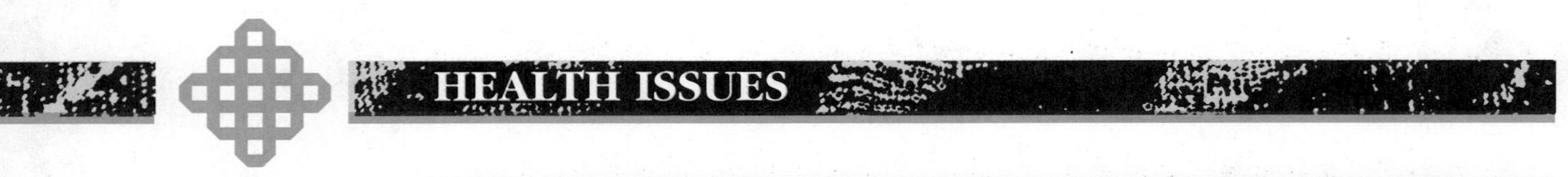

Lesson 7: Expressing Ability, and Making General Requests, Predictions, and Inferences

PREVIEW

Check all of the following activities you do regularly (at least 30 minutes three to five days a week):

Strenuous Activity	*Moderate Activity*
_____ run/jog	_____ garden
_____ bike	_____ rake leaves
_____ swim	_____ vacuum
_____ do aerobics	_____ shoot baskets
_____ play tennis (singles)	_____ push the lawn mower
_____ play squash/raquetball	_____ take a brisk walk
_____ play basketball	_____ go up and down stairs

EXERCISE: HOW MUCH IS ENOUGH?

"Continuous, strenuous **exertion** is *not* necessary for good health. Just 30 minutes of moderate, **intermittent** exercise at least four days a week is an acceptable alternative for people who don't think of themselves as exercise **enthusiasts**."* If you can take the stairs instead of the elevator, take a brisk walk during your lunch break, garden, rake leaves, vacuum, push the lawn mower, or shoot baskets, you will get moderate exercise—and without any special equipment. In contrast, the old guidelines recommended 20 to 60 minutes of nonstop aerobic exercise at least three to five times a week.

"Many people will look at these new recommendations and say, 'Hey, I'm doing that,' but they aren't," warns Russell Pate of the American College of Sports Medicine. "You've got to **accumulate** 30 minutes of moderate activity over the course of most days of the week." Unfortunately, most Americans must prefer the couch: nearly 80 percent don't get enough exercise.

From "A New Exercise Alternative? Experts Say They Made a Mistake." *Hope Health Letter,* (Dec. 1993), Vol. 13(12). Published by the Hope Heart Institute, Seattle, Washington.

*According to new guidelines released by the Centers for Disease Control and Prevention, The American College of Sports Medicine, and the President's Council on Physical Fitness.

exertion exercise, strong effort
intermittent stopping and starting at intervals, not continuous
enthusiast a person who is intensely involved in a particular activity or subject
accumulate add up, increase over time

All except one of the underlined words are from a group of auxiliaries called **modals.** The remaining expanded verb is a **semimodal,** a special expression that can be used in place of a modal. Can you find it?_______________

PRESENTATION

Modals occur in both speech and writing, but they are especially common in speech. Modals are sometimes difficult to learn for three reasons: (1) many of them can be used in both present (now) and past (then) time frames; (2) they have different, but often overlapping, meanings; and (3) they can express different degrees of politeness. **Semimodals** can be used in place of some modals (e.g., be able to, have to, ought to). They are similar in meaning but not in form to modals.

The form of modals is easy: they always occur as **modal + base** form of the verb. However, not all modals can be used in both now and then time frames. Table 2.1 shows which time frame you can use the modals in.

Table 2.1 Time Frames the Modals Can Be Used In

Now	will would	can could	shall should	may might	must
Then	would	could	should	might	

The meaning of modals often varies. Table 2.2 lists the different modals that can be used to express ability, make general requests, predictions, and inferences. As the table shows, not all modals have semimodals that are similar in meaning to them.

Table 2.2. Expressing Ability, Making General Requests, and Making Predictions and Inferences

MEANING	MODAL		SEMIMODAL
Ability	can	could	BE able to
General Requests	can will	could would	
Predictions (stating what will happen in the future)	will	would	BE going to BE about to (for immediate future only)
Inferences (making educated guesses)	may must	might could	

Ability

1. I **can** play tennis for two hours without a break.
2. Last year I **could** play for three hours without stopping.
3. By the end of the summer I'**ll be able** to play longer again.
   NOT: I'**ll can** play longer again.

General Requests

1. (To a friend) **Can** you show me how you throw curve balls?
2. (To a pro ball player) **Would** you sign this baseball?
3. (To a sales person) **Could** you tell me the difference between these two bats?
4. (To a team member) Hey, **give** me that ball!

Different modals express varying degrees of politeness, from polite to direct. Using an imperative form (base form), as in sentence #4, is the most direct way to request.

Figure. 2.1 shows the polite-to-direct continuum for general requests.

FIGURE 2.1 Modals for Making General Requests

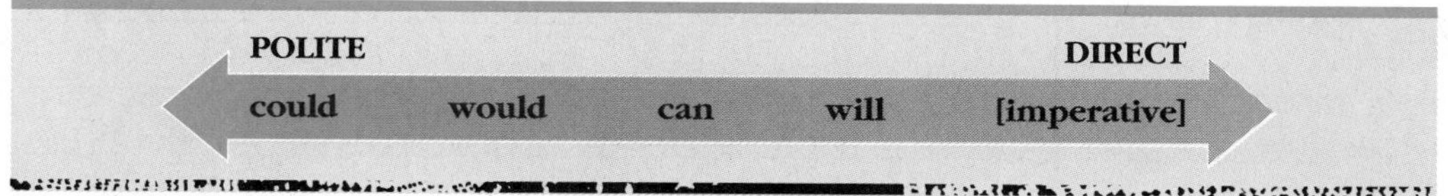

Predictions

1. The next World Cup games <u>will</u> be in 1998.
2. The teams from Brazil and Italy <u>should</u> easily qualify to play.
3. The U.S. team <u>could</u> qualify (it's possible but not likely).

Different modals express different degrees of certainty in predictions. Figure 2.2 shows this continuum:

FIGURE 2.2 Modals for Making Predictions

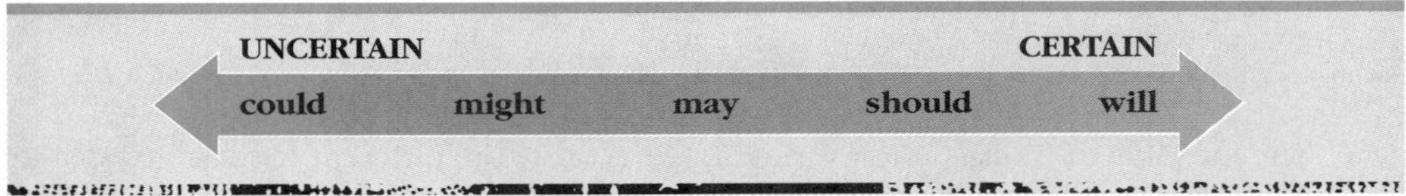

Inferences:

1. The phone is still ringing. My friend <u>must</u> not be home.
2. She <u>may</u> be on her way to meet me.
3. Or she <u>could</u> be waiting for me at the game.

These modals also form a continuum from uncertain to certain, as Figure 2.3 shows.

FIGURE 2.3 Modals for Making Inferences

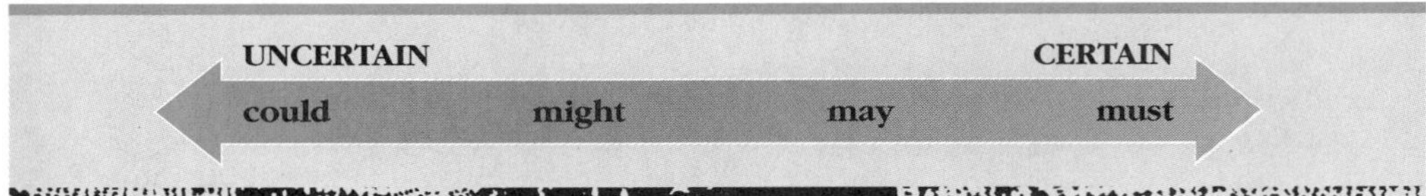

For more information about modals and semimodals, see *The Tapestry Grammar,* Chapter. 8, pages 191–204.

PRACTICE

Activity 1

Choose a sport/activity that you like or do well. Then divide up the sport/activity into smaller skills/abilities. Write three sentences telling what you can/can't do now or will/won't be able to do in the future. The first item is an example for you.

1. Sport/Activity: running
   Skills/Abilities: stretching, jogging, running fast for 10 minutes, running a four-minute mile, cooling down
   I can jog 5K now.
   I can't run a four-minute mile.
   After four weeks of training, I'll be able to jog for 10K.

2. Sport/Activity: ____________________
   Skills/Abilities: ____________________
   ____
   ____
   ____

3. Sport/Activity: ______________________

Skills/Abilities: ______________________

____

____

____

Activity 2

Partners. Find someone in your class who does the same or a similar sport/activity as you described in Activity 1. Ask your partner questions about the skills/abilities he or she has now, using **can,** and about the skills/abilities he or she expects to have in the future, using **will be able to**. You may want to write down your partner's answers so you can report them to the class.

Activity 3

Imagine that you have decided to play a new sport, take up a new musical instrument, or start a new hobby. Decide what you want to do and then make a list of any special equipment, clothing, or materials you need to get started. Choose one or more of the following activities to complete:

1. A friend of yours is very good at what you want to do. Write a dialogue between you and your friend in which you request some information about equipment, clothing, or materials you may need.
2. Write a second version of the dialogue in (1), this time between you and a salesperson at a store that sells the equipment, clothing, or materials you need.
3. Call up a local store and request information about the equipment, clothing, or materials you need. You may find it helpful to first practice an open-ended dialogue with a partner in which you ask questions that he or she has never heard before.

Activity 4

Individuals/partners. The water in your home is going to be shut off for 24 to 48 hours because of contamination (an impurity) in the water supply. Write at least one answer to each of the questions. You may find it helpful to refer to Figures 2.1 to 2.3 in this lesson first.

1. What could you do? ______________________

   ____

2. What might you do? ______________________

   ____

3. What may you do? ______________________

   ____

4. What should you do? ______________________

   ____

5. What will you do? ______________________

   ____

6. What else are you going to do? ______________________

   ____

   ____

Compare your answers to your partners' answers; be prepared to defend your answers. For example, why **won't** you do all the things you **could** do? Why **should** you do some things? What makes you uncertain about some things you **might** do?

Activity 5.

Individuals/partners. Is it influenza (the flu) or a cold? Sometimes the symptoms are confusing. Read Table 2.3. Then write sentences that make inferences about whether the person has the flu or a cold. Your inferences may differ in degree of certainty (see Figure 2.3). The first one is done for you.

Table 2.3 Is It a Cold or the Flu?

	CHECK THESE SYMPTOMS	
SYMPTOMS	**COLD**	**FLU**
Fever	Rare	Characteristic, high (102–104°F) sudden onset; lasts three to four days.
Headache	Rare	Prominent
General aches and pains	Rare	Usual; often quite severe
Fatigue, weakness	Slight	Extreme; can last two to three weeks
Total exhaustion	Never	Early and prominent
Runny, stuffy nose	Common	Sometimes
Sneezing	Usual	Sometimes
Sore throat	Common	Sometimes
Chest discomfort, cough	Mild to moderate hacking cough	Common, can become severe

Source: Beloit College, *News from the Health Center* (December 1993).

1. A high fever *You must have the flu.*
2. A severe headache ______
3. General aches and pains ______
4. Fatigue, weakness for a few days ______
5. Total exhaustion ______
6. Runny, stuffy nose ______
7. Frequent sneezing ______
8. Sore throat ______
9. Moderate cough ______

Oral practice.

Describe your symptoms to a partner. Your partner tries to decide whether you have a cold or the flu.

Lesson 8: Expressing Permission, Recommendation, and Obligation

PREVIEW

CHECK YOUR EMERGENCY IQ

Test yourself. Circle the letter before the correct answer. Before you begin, you may find it helpful to check the vocabulary listed after these questions.

1. Your three-year-old son has just swallowed **charcoal fluid.** You should immediately
   a. call the poison control center.
   b. feed him **syrup of ipecac.**
   c. take him to the emergency room.

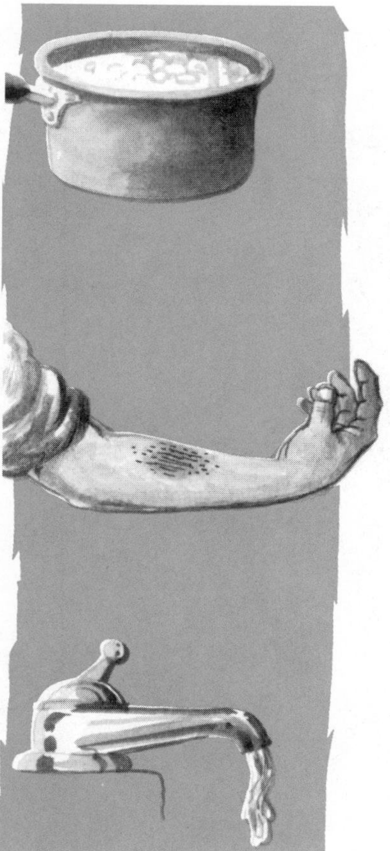

2. You're visiting your father-in-law when he suddenly falls to the floor, **unconscious** and without a **pulse.** What should you do?
   a. dial **911.**
   b. begin **cardiopulmonary resuscitation (CPR),** including mouth-to-mouth resuscitation and chest-pumping.
3. You **spill** boiling water and badly burn your arm. You should
   a. wrap ice cubes in cloth and hold them on the burn for 10 minutes.
   b. run cold water on the burn for 10 minutes.
   c. rub cold butter into the burn.
4. You've just pulled your five-year-old niece from the swimming pool. She is unconscious and doesn't have a pulse. You should
   a. begin CPR immediately.
   b. run to dial 911 then attempt CPR.
5. Your husband badly **sprains** his ankle playing basketball in the backyard. You should help him to
   a. soak his ankle in hot water.
   b. lie down with his ankle elevated above his head and wrapped in ice.
   c. walk around quickly to keep the blood circulating.
6. A friend who is **diabetic** is walking around a picnic area acting drunk, yet has had only one beer. You should
   a. take him immediately to the hospital before he falls into a diabetic **coma.**
   b. get him to take his **insulin.**
   c. feed him juice or a soft drink.

Adapted from Valerie Fahey, "Check Your Emergency IQ," *Health,* July–August 1994, Vol. 8 (4).

charcoal fluid flammable liquid used to start charcoal fires
syrup of ipecac liquid used to make someone vomit in case of poisoning
unconscious loss of awareness, temporary loss of sensory perception (hearing, sight, touch, etc.)
pulse heartbeat
911 the rapid-response emergency phone number to call in many U.S. communities
cardiopulmonary resuscitation (CPR) a procedure used to restart breathing and circulation after the heart stops
spill cause or allow something to run or fall out of a container
sprain painfully twist the ligaments of a joint or muscle
diabetic a person with diabetes, a chronic disease characterized by a deficiency of insulin
coma deep unconsciousness, usually from injury, disease, or poison
insulin a hormone that controls blood sugar levels in the body

Check your answers

1. **a** Definitely have syrup of ipecac on hand in case you need to induce vomiting, but don't use any poison remedy without first checking. In this case, vomiting could force the gas into the boy's lungs or injure his esophagus. The poison center will ask the boy's symptoms and help you decide whether to get him to a hospital or just let the fluid pass naturally through his digestive tract.
2. **a** Because cardiac arrest in adults is usually caused by ventricular fibrillation, in which the heart's electrical signals go haywire, CPR is rarely effective. It saves lives only one in ten times. Starting CPR after the 911 call is recommended, but the top priority is to get the defibrillator machine carried by most emergency teams to your father-in-law's side.
3. **b** Though butter and ice were once recommended for burns, they're now no-nos. Ice can further damage the skin, while butter is just ineffective. After running water on a burn, seek medical attention for blistered, charred, or peeling burns.
4. **a** Usually a child's heart stops because he or she isn't getting air, so the top priority here is CPR. Give one mouth-to-mouth breath and pump her chest every three seconds for at least one minute before carrying her to the phone to dial 911. Then try CPR again.
5. **b** Do everything contained in the acronym RICE—rest, ice, compression (with an Ace bandage), and elevation. If swelling hasn't gone down at all in 48 hours, call a doctor; the injury could require a cast.
6. **c** Low blood sugar due to too much insulin or not enough food can cause incoherence in a diabetic. With the sugar in four ounces of juice or soft drink, or alternatively, a candy bar, he should be back to normal in 15 minutes. If he's still shaky, a bit more sugar might be needed.

If you got any wrong, you might want to pick up a resource book at the local bookstore. A good one is *Emergency Medical Treatment,* by Stephen Vogel and David Manhoff, Willmette, Illinois; EMT, Inc., 1993. Another good source (of classes as well as information) is your local chapter of the American Red Cross.

Valerie Fahey, *Health,* July–August 1994. Reprinted by permission.

How did you do? You may want to take the author's advice and pick up a first-aid book if you got any answers wrong. Take a look at the answers again. Circle all the **modals.** Did you find all eight?

PRESENTATION

In addition to the meanings discussed in Lesson 7, **modals** and **semimodals** are used to describe actions that are allowed (permission), suggested (recommendation), or required (obligation). These modals are used most often when you are talking, and all (even the "past" forms) refer to present time (now). Table 2.4 lists the modals and semimodals used to express permission, recommendation, and obligation. Not all modals have corresponding semimodals.

TABLE 2.4 Expressing Permission, Recommendation, and Obligation

MEANING	MODAL	SEMIMODAL
Permission	may or can	
Recommendation	should had better	ought to (mainly British English)
Obligation	must	have to have got to (mainly British)

Permission

1. May I ask you a question? (more formal)
2. Can I take this medication on an empty stomach? (less formal)
3. Yes, you can. It doesn't cause stomach upset or nausea.

Recommendation

1. If you have a sore throat, try a home treatment. For pain relief, you could take aspirin or acetaminophen.
2. You might eat a popsicle or have a cold drink.
3. With children, you should only use acetaminophen. (Aspirin is associated with Reye's syndrome in children.)
4. You had better see a doctor if you have great difficulty in swallowing (or you could get really sick).

Had better makes a stronger recommendation than should. If a recommendation with had better is not followed, a negative consequence is usually understood or stated, as in sentence #4.

Obligation/Lack of Obligation

1. If someone is in shock, you must act immediately.
2. You must not move anybody with a neck or back injury unless it is absolutely necessary.
3. Someone has to call for help.
4. You don't have to know first aid to dial 911.

Both **must** and **must not** express an obligation (to do something and *not* to do something). **Have to** also expresses obligation and is less formal than **must/must not**. When there is no obligation, **not have to** is used, as in sentence #4.

These **modals** and **semimodals** form a continuum from "permission" (most free) to "obligation" (least free), as Figure. 2.4 shows.

FIGURE 2.4 Modals for Permission, Recommendation, and Obligation

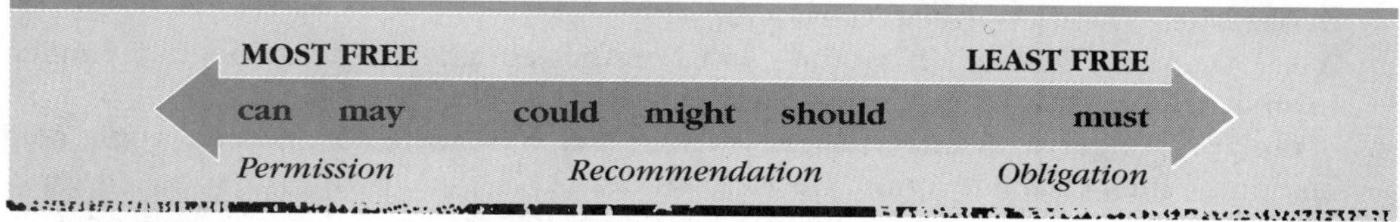

For further information about modals and semimodals, see *The Tapestry Grammar,* Chapter 8, pages 191–204.

PRACTICE

Activity 1

Partners. Match the following emergency situations and symptoms with the appropriate treatment by writing the letter of the appropriate treatment in the blank. Check your answers with a partner.

_____ **1.** Appendicitis. Pain in right lower abdomen. Nausea, possibly vomiting. Low fever. Constipation.

_____ **2.** Choking. Inability to breathe, cough, or speak. Bluish lips, nails, or skin.

_____ **3.** Cuts and bruises. Cuts: Injuries to skin with bleeding and pain. Bruises: Redness on impact, then black and blue.

_____ **4.** Dog bite. Deep bleeding, painful wound. Major danger is rabies, which can be fatal.

_____ **5.** Drowning. Unconsciousness. Not breathing, possibly no heartbeat. Cold exposure. Shock.

_____ **6.** Fractures and dislocations. Severe pain, swelling or bruising. Loss of motion. Protruding bone.

_____ **7.** Frostbite. Area (usually extremities) becomes red, then gray, then white. Numbness (lack of feeling).

_____ **8.** Insect bites and stings. Pain. Itching. Swelling. Redness. If allergic: Difficulty breathing, swallowing.

_____ **9.** Poisoning. Vomiting or diarrhea. Sweating. Convulsions. Unconsciousness.

_____ **10.** Shock. Pale, clammy skin. Weakness. Fast breathing. Rapid, weak pulse. Confusion.

ASK·A·NURSE®
Rockford
Memorial Hospital
968-1999

Treatment

a. Don't move if unconscious or if back/neck injuries suspected. Treat breathing/bleeding/shock first. Immobilize injury before moving.
b. Lay on back with feet raised unless you supect head/back injuries. Check for breathing/bleeding difficulties. Call for help.
c. Cuts: Stop bleeding with direct pressure; clean with soap/water; cover with sterile bandage. Bruises: apply cold packs; elevate affected arm or leg.
d. Control bleeding. Wash with soap/water. Identify animal; call authorities for rabies check. Call doctor.
e. Call doctor immediately. While diagnosis is uncertain, don't give anything to eat or drink. Don't use laxatives or pain medications.
f. Call regional poison control center IMMEDIATELY. Report victim's condition and nearest hospital. Follow orders. Collect vomit/urine.
g. Don't rub. Slowly warm by putting in tepid (not hot) water. Give warm drinks and wrap in blankets. When rewarmed, call doctor.
h. Ask: "Are you choking?" If victim can't breathe, cough, or speak, begin Heimlich maneuver. (See Lesson 9 for instructions.)
i. Scrape off stinger with fingernail, don't squeeze. Wash with soap/water. Apply cold compress, then calamine lotion. Get help IMMEDIATELY if allergic.
j. If not breathing, begin mouth-to-mouth breathing. Call for help. If no pulse, begin CPR (if trained). Elevate feet, keep warm.

LEARNING STRATEGY

Overcoming Limitations: Trying to use the context will help you understand new vocabulary before you use a dictionary.

Activity 2.

Partners. Write a short dialogue between a caller with a health problem listed in Activity 1 and a nurse on the ASK-A-NURSE Hotline. Describe the symptoms and make appropriate recommendations. Roleplay the call and change roles so that each of you can give advice.

Activity 3.

Read about things to include in a first-aid kit. Then write sentences telling what you **may/can** do with an item and sentences telling what you **should/had better** do. Two sentences are done for you as examples

Things to include in a basic first-aid kit.

Making a First-Aid Kit

FRAGRANCE-FREE SOAP to clean hands and wounds.

PAIN-RELIEF TABLETS and children's acetaminophen elixer.

ANGLE-EDGE TWEEZERS to pluck glass and splinters.

ADHESIVE-STRIP BANDAGES.

STERILE FOUR-INCH GAUZE PADS long gauze roll, and tape.

SCISSORS.

COTTON-TIP APPLICATORS and cotton balls.

ANTIHISTAMINE CREAM for insect bites and itching.

STRETCH FABRIC BANDAGE for sprains.

FLASHLIGHT.

ORAL THERMOMETER.

OLD CREDIT CARD to scrape bee stings.

DISPOSABLE LATEX GLOVES.

"INSTANT ICE" COMPRESS.

BETADINE painless disinfecting wound cleanser.

BACITRACIN or other multiple antibiotic ointment for minor cuts.

IPECAC SYRUP and activated charcoal for poison antidotes (call a poison control center immediately).

ISOPROPYL ALCOHOL and antiseptic towelettes.

AMMONIA INHALANT.

CALAMINE LOTION.

TELEPHONE NUMBERS for doctor and poison control center.

Source: From Deborah Hofman, "For a First-Aid Kit, Forget Caboodle," *The New York Times,* July 8, 1993. Reprinted by permission.

May/can

1. *You can clean hands and wounds with fragrance-free soap.*
2. ______
3. ______
4. ______
5. ______

Should/had better

1. *You should clean a wound before you put on any bandage.*
2. ______
3. ______
4. ______
5. ______

Activity 4.

Read the rules for children who participate in the Safe Place Program, an after-school program for children ages 5 to 12. Rewrite the rules so that they are more informal, for example, what you might say to a child. Use semimodals or less formal modals. You may want to change some other words, too, as in sentence #1:

1. To participate, children must register first and everyone must sign in. *You have to register first and everyone has to sign in before you can come to Safe Place.*

2. Participants must be free of contagious diseases and physically fit to join in activities. ______________________________

3. Participants must stay in assigned areas. ______________________________

4. Participants are advised to show respect for themselves, for others, and the Center by being polite to other children and adults. ______________________________

5. Participants may leave whenever they wish to go, but they will be asked to leave if they are not following rules. ______________________________

6. If participants are asked to leave, they may not return that day. ______________________________

7. Adults are at the Center to help. Be sure to inform them of any problems. ______________________________

Activity 5.

Read the following health regulations in Table 2.5 about travel from the United States to other countries. Then write a short paragraph that summarizes what travelers **must/have to, may/can/be able to,** or **not have to** do to visit these countries. Try to use a variety of modals and semimodals.

TABLE 2.5 Vaccination Recommendations for Travel Abroad

COUNTRY	REQUIRED HEALTH PROCEDURES	RECOMMENDED HEALTH PROCEDURES
Ecuador	Yellow fever shot, if coming from an infected area	1. Mefloquine pills to protect against malaria 2. Cholera shot 3. Tetanus booster shot
Japan	No vaccinations required	Tetanus booster shot
Zimbabwe	Yellow fever shot, if coming from an infected area	1. Mefloquine pills to protect against malaria 2. Cholera shot 3. Tetanus booster shot 4. Typhoid shot 5. Gamma globulin to protect against hepatitis A 6. Hepatitis B shots (3) 7. Oral polio booster

NOTE The United States is not considered an infected area for malaria.

From guidelines published by the Centers for Disease Contol, and Prevention, Atlanta, Georgia, June 1995.

Lesson 9: Modals: Describing Real Expectations and Imagined Situations in the Present (*If*-Clauses)

PREVIEW

Choking (stopping breathing because of a blocked air passage) can happen to anyone. Have you ever helped someone who was choking? Do you know how to do the Heimlich manuever? If you don't, here's what to do:

THE HEIMLICH MANEUVER* FOR CHOKING

STEP 1. Ask: "Are you choking?"

STEP 2. If the victim can't breathe, cough, or speak, begin the Heimlich maneuver:

Stand behind the choking victim.
Wrap your arms around the victim's **waist** and lock your hands into a **fist.**
Place the thumbside of your fist against the victim's **abdomen,** slightly above the **navel** and below the **rib cage.**
Press your fist into the victim's abdomen with a quick upward thrust.

STEP 3. Repeat thrust if necessary.

*The Heimlich maneuver was named after Dr. Henry J. Heimlich, a twentieth-century U.S. surgeon.

waist the part of the torso between the rib cage and the navel
fist the hand with the fingers tightly closed
abdomen stomach
navel on mammals, the mark on the stomach where the umbilical cord was attached; also known informally as the "belly button"
rib cage the circular bone structure formed by the ribs

The following sentence is an example of a **conditional clause** (the *if* clause) with a **real expectation** (the main clause), which is likely to come true:

If people are prepared, they can act appropriately in an emergency

There are two other examples of conditional clauses with real expectations in the Preview. Can you find them?

1. ______________________________

2. ______________________________

PRESENTATION

Real expectations. Think about these sentences:

1. If you <u>eat</u> like most Americans, you <u>will</u> gain about six pounds during the holidays (Thanksgiving to New Year's).
2. If you <u>limit</u> your fat intake to 30 percent of your total calories, you <u>can</u> consume up to 67 g of fat.*
3. If you <u>eat</u> 1/2 cup of peanuts, you <u>use</u> 35 g of fat.
4. If you <u>eat</u> 1 cup of ice cream, you <u>use</u> 14 g of fat. It's not hard to use up a whole day's allowance of fat with snacks and dessert!

*Based on a 2,000-calorie diet.

The *if* clauses in sentences #1 to #4 describe conditions in the present in which the **expected consequence** (the main clause) is likely to happen. That's why these sentences are sometimes called **real** conditional sentences: if the condition occurs, the consequence is expected to come true. In sentences describing real expectations, the verb or modal in the *if* clause is in the present (now time frame), and so is the verb or modal in the main clause. Figure 2.5 shows how the present time forms in the *if* clause relate to the modal in the main clause.

FIGURE 2.5 Verbs and Modals in *if* Sentences: Real Expectations

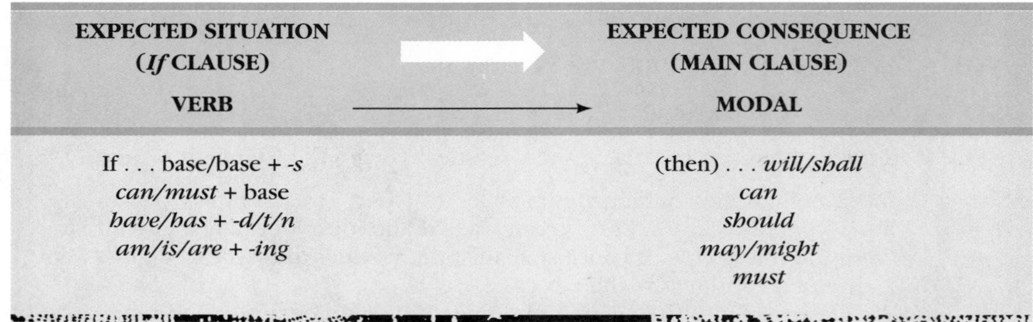

EXPECTED SITUATION (*If* CLAUSE) VERB	EXPECTED CONSEQUENCE (MAIN CLAUSE) MODAL
If . . . base/base + *-s*	(then) . . . *will/shall*
can/must + base	*can*
have/has + *-d/t/n*	*should*
am/is/are + *-ing*	*may/might*
	must

NOTE

1. Though you can use various kinds of present tense verbs in the *if* clause, *can* and *must* are the only modals that can be used there. The most common form in the *if* clause is the simple verb (base or base + *-s*).
2. *Will* is by far the most common modal in the main clause.
3. It is also possible to use a simple present tense verb in the main clause if you are describing some habitual activity.
4. In an *if* sentence that describes real expectations, you can never use *would* or *could,* either in the *if* clause or in the main clause.

If no **modal** is used in the main clause, it is also possible to use the imperative form:

If you are trying to lose weight, don't eat peanuts.

Imagined Situations. In imagined situations, the *if* clause describes an event that hasn't happened and is not likely to happen (at least not in the near future). The **imagined consequence** (the main clause) hasn't happened either, but it can be imagined. That's why these sentences are sometimes called **unreal** or **contrary-to-fact**: because the condition isn't true, the consequence isn't true either.

1. If Americans knew the fat content in the food they eat, they would change their eating habits. (In fact, they don't know the fat content.)
2. If Americans just tried to maintain their weight during the holidays (instead of dieting), they might succeed. (In fact, they don't try to maintain their weight.)

In sentences describing imagined situations in the present, the verb or modal in both the *if* clause and the main clause is in the *past* (then time frame). That is, the verb or modal backshifts to the *past* to indicate unreal conditions in the *present*. Figure 2.6 shows how the past forms in the *if* clause relate to the modal in the main clause.

FIGURE 2.6 Verbs and Modals in *if* Sentences: Imagined Situations

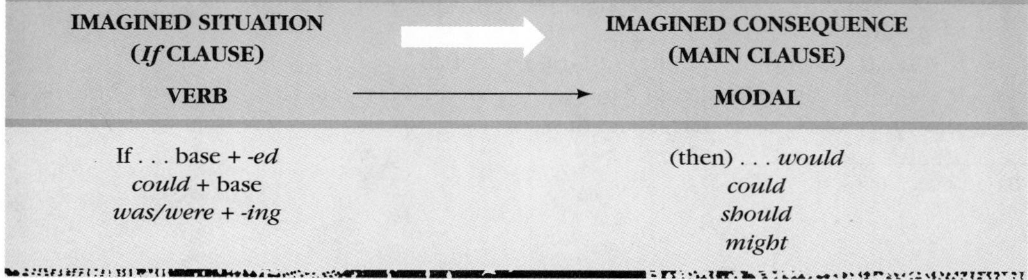

IMAGINED SITUATION (*If* CLAUSE) VERB	IMAGINED CONSEQUENCE (MAIN CLAUSE) MODAL
If . . . base + *-ed*	(then) . . . *would*
could + base	*could*
was/were + *-ing*	*should*
	might

Grammar note. Imagined situations can be described using *if* clauses or **verbal phrases.** Verbal phrases have no tense, but the fact that they refer to imagined situations is understood when **would** occurs in the clause that follows. In the first sentence, the verbal phrase is in italic. The equivalent sentence with an *if* clause follows.

- *Knowing the fat content of the food you eat,* would you change your eating habits?
- If you knew the fat content of the food you eat, would you change your eating habits?

For additional information about verbal phrases in imagined situations, see *The Tapestry Grammar,* Chapter 8, page 197.

PRACTICE

Activity 1

Oral or written practice (partners). Read the following flowchart for treating sore throats and the list of suggested home treatments that follow. Go over any vocabulary that is new to you. Then, with a partner practice making up sentences with real conditions and expected consequences. The first sentence is an example for you.

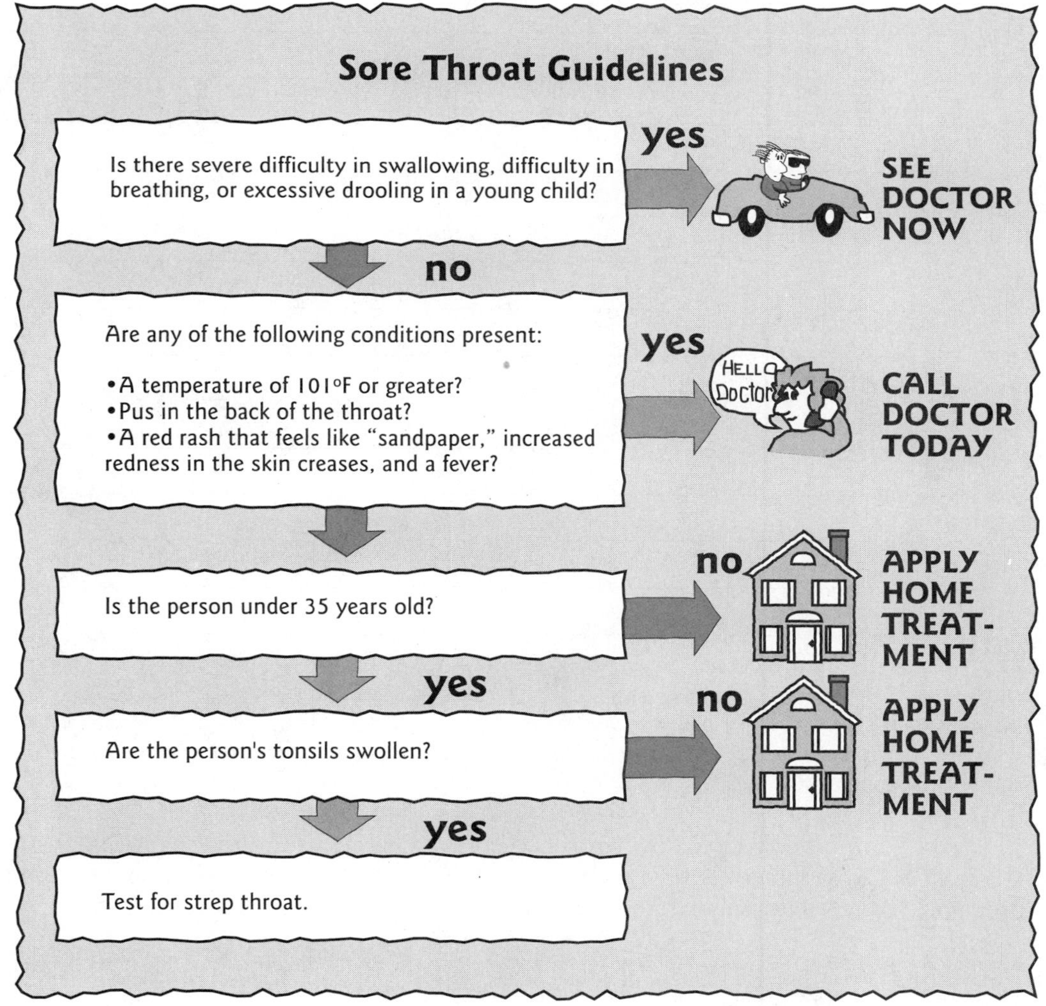

Hope Health Letter, December 1993, Vol. 13 (12). Hope Heart Institute, Seattle, WA. Reprinted by permission.

drool saliva that runs from the mouth
pus a thick yellowish-white liquid that is a sign of infection
rash an eruption (bumps) on the skin or in the mouth
sandpaper heavy paper coated on one side with sand or an abrasive material to smooth surfaces
tonsils two tissues that are located in the back of the throat on the sides; they may become inflamed (swollen) or infected
strep a type of bacteria from the strain *streptococcus* that can cause disease

Home Treatments

Popsicles	Vaporizer
Cold liquids	Throat lozenges
Aspirin or acetaminophen (for example, Tylenol)	Saltwater gargle (1/4 tsp. salt to two cups warm water)

1. *If you have great difficulty in swallowing, you should see a doctor immediately.*

2.

3.

4.

5.

6.

Activity 2.

Read the following Nutrition Facts from four popular breakfast cereals and then answer the questions.

FOR YOUR INFORMATION North Americans often eat cold cereal for breakfast. In 1994 the U.S. government developed new nutrition labels that must appear on most food products. "Daily Value" refers to the recommended daily allowance of a nutrient.

A

LOW-FAT CEREAL

Nutrition Facts

Serving Size 2/3 Cup (55g/2.0 oz.)
Servings Per Container 11

Amount Per Serving	Cereal	Cereal with 1/2 Cup Vitamins A&D Skim Milk
Calories	210	250
Fat Calories	30	30
	% Daily Value**	
Total Fat 3.0g*	**5** %	**5** %
Saturated Fat 0g	**0** %	**0** %
Cholesterol 0mg	**0** %	**0** %
Sodium 135mg	**6** %	**8** %
Potassium 160mg	**5** %	**10** %
Total Carbohydrate 43g	**14** %	**16** %
Dietary Fiber 3g	**12** %	**12** %
Sugars 16g		
Other Carbohydrate 24g		
Protein 5g		
Vitamin A	15 %	20 %
Vitamin C	0 %	2 %
Calcium	2 %	15 %
Iron	10 %	10 %
Vitamin D	10 %	25 %
Vitamin E	25 %	25 %
Thiamin	25 %	30 %
Riboflavin	25 %	35 %
Niacin	25 %	25 %
Vitamin B_6	25 %	25 %
Folate	25 %	25 %
Vitamin B_{12}	25 %	35 %
Phosphorus	15 %	25 %
Magnesium	10 %	15 %
Zinc	25 %	30 %
Copper	6 %	8 %

* Amount in cereal. One half cup of skim milk contributes an additional 65mg sodium, 6g total carbohydrate (6g sugars), and 4g protein.

** Percent Daily Values are based on a 2,000 calorie diet. Your daily values may be higher or lower depending on you calorie needs:

	Calories:	2,000	2,500
Total Fat	Less than	65g	80g
Sat. Fat	Less than	20g	25g
Cholesterol	Less than	300mg	300mg
Sodium	Less than	2,400mg	2,400mg
Potassium		3,500mg	3,500mg
Total Carbohydrate		300g	375g
Dietary Fiber		25g	30g

Calories Per Gram:
Fat 9 • Carbohydrate 4 • Protein 4

Ingredients: Whole grain oats and whole grain wheat, brown sugar, raisins, rice, corn syrup, almonds, glycerin, partially hydrogenated cottonseed and/or soybean oil, modified corn starch, salt, cinnamon, nonfat dry milk, polyglycerol esters, malt flavoring. **Vitamins and Minerals:** alpha tocopherol acetate (vitamin E), niacinamide, zinc oxide, iron, pyridoxine hydrochloride (vitamin B_6), riboflavin (vitamin B_2), vitamin A palmitate (protected with BHT), thiamin hydrochloride (vitamin B_1), folic acid, vitamin B_{12} and vitamin D.

B

Nutrition Facts

Serving Size 3/4 cup (32g)
Servings Per Container about 19
Amount Per Serving

Amount Per Serving	Cereal Alone	with 1/2 Cup Vitamin A&D Fortified Skim Milk
Calories	120	160
Calories from Fat	15	15
	% Daily Value**	
Total Fat 1.5g*	**2%**	**2%**
Saturated Fat 0g	**0%**	**0%**
Polyunsaturated Fat 0.5g		
Monounsaturated Fat 0.5g		
Cholesterol 0mg	**0%**	**0%**
Sodium 170mg	**7%**	**10%**
Potassium 80mg	**2%**	**8%**
Total Carbohydrate 25g	**8%**	**10%**
Other Carbohydrate 17g		
Dietary Fiber 2g	**8%**	**8%**
Sugars 6g		
Protein 3g		
Vitamin A	***	4%
Vitamin C	***	2%
Calcium	8%	20%
Iron	45%	50%
Thiamin	25%	25%
Riboflavin	25%	35%
Niacin	25%	25%
Vitamin B_6	25%	25%
Folate	25%	25%
Phosphorus	10%	20%
Zinc	25%	25%

* Amount in Cereal. One-half cup skim milk contributes an additional 40 Calories, 65mg Sodium, 6g Total Carbohydrate (6g Sugars), and 4g Protein.

** Percent Daily Values are based on a 2,000 calorie diet. Your daily values may be higher or lower depending on you calorie needs.

*** Contains less than 2% of the daily value of these nutrients.

	Calories:	2,000	2,500
Total Fat	Less than	65g	80g
Sat Fat	Less than	20g	25g
Cholesterol	Less than	300mg	300mg
Sodium	Less than	2,400mg	2,400mg
Total Carbohydrate		300mg	375g
Dietary Fiber		25g	30g
Potassium		3,500mg	3,500mg

Calories Per Gram:
Fat 9 • Carbohydrate 4 • Protein 4

Ingredients: Whole oat flour (with oat bran), sugar, rice flour, corn flour, whole wheat flour, high starch oat flour, salt, calcium carbonate, sodium phosphate (a phosphorus source and dough conditioner), reduced iron, niacinamide*, zinc oxide (a source of zinc), BHT (a preservative), yellow 5, yellow 6, pyridoxine hydrochloride*, thiamin mononitrate*, riboflavin*, folic acid*.
*One of the B vitamins.

C

Nutrition Facts

Serving Size 1 cup (30g/1.1 oz.)
Servings Per Container 17

Amount Per Serving	Cereal	with 1/2 Cup Vitamin A&D Skim Milk
Calories	110	150
Fat Calories	0	0
	% Daily Value**	
Total Fat 0g*	**0** %	**0** %
Saturated Fat 0g	**0** %	**0** %
Cholesterol 0mg	**0** %	**0** %
Sodium 330mg	**14** %	**16** %
Potassium 35mg	**1** %	**7** %
Total Carbohydrate 26g	**9** %	**11** %
Dietary Fiber 1g	**4** %	**4** %
Sugars 2g		
Other Carbohydrate 23g		
Protein 2g		
Vitamin A	15 %	20 %
Vitamin C	25 %	25 %
Calcium	0 %	15 %
Iron	45 %	45 %
Vitamin D	10 %	25 %
Thiamin	25 %	30 %
Riboflavin	25 %	35 %
Niacin	25 %	25 %
Vitamin B_6	25 %	25 %
Folate	25 %	25 %

* Amount in Cereal. One half cup skim milk contributes an additional 40 calories, 65mg sodium, 6g total carbohydrate (6g sugars), and 4g Protein.

** Percent Daily Values are based on a 2,000 calorie diet. Your daily values may be higher or lower depending on you calorie needs.

	Calories:	2,000	2,500
Total Fat	Less than	65g	80g
Sat Fat	Less than	20g	25g
Cholesterol	Less than	300mg	300mg
Sodium	Less than	2,400mg	2,400mg
Potassium		3,500mg	3,500mg
Total Carbohydrate		300mg	375g
Dietary Fiber		25g	30g

Calories Per Gram:
Fat 9 • Carbohydrate 4 • Protein 4

Ingredients: Corn, sugar, salt, malt flavoring, corn syrup, **Vitamins and Iron:** ascorbic acid (vitamin C), iron, niacinamide, pyridoxine hydrochloride (vitamin B_6), riboflavin (vitamin B_2), vitamin A palmitate, thiamin hydrochloride (vitamin B_1), folic acid, and vitamin D. To maintain quality, BHT has been added to the packaging.

D

Nutrition Facts

Serving Size 1 Cup (30g)
Servings Per Container About 14

Amount Per Serving	Cereal	with 1/2 Cup Skim milk
Calories	110	150
Calories from Fat	15	20
		% Daily Value**
Total Fat 2g*	3%	3%
Saturated Fat 0g	0%	0%
Cholesterol 0mg	0%	1%
Sodium 280mg	12%	14%
Potassium 90mg	3%	8%
Total Carbohydrate 22g	7%	9%
Dietary Fiber 3g	11%	11%
Sugars 1g		
Other Carbohydrate 18g		
Protein 3g		
Vitamin A	25%	30%
Vitamin C	25%	25%
Calcium	4%	20%
Iron	45%	45%
Vitamin D	10%	25%
Thiamin	25%	30%
Riboflavin	25%	35%
Niacin	25%	25%
Vitamin B_6	25%	25%
Folic Acid	25%	25%
Phosphorus	10%	20%
Magnesium	6%	10%
Zinc	25%	30%
Copper	2%	2%

*Amount in Cereal. A serving of cereal plus skim milk provides 2g fat,<5mg cholesterol, 340mg sodium, 290mg potassium, 28g carbohydrate (7g sugars) and 7g protein.

**Percent Daily Values are based on a 2,000 calorie diet. Your daily values may be higher or lower depending on you calorie needs.

	Calories:	2,000	2,500
Total Fat	Less than	65g	80g
Sat. Fat	Less than	20g	25g
Cholesterol	Less than	300mg	300mg
Sodium	Less than	2,400mg	2,400mg
Potassium		3,500mg	3,500mg
Total Carbohydrate		300g	375g
Dietary Fiber		25g	30g

INGREDIENTS: WHOLE OAT FLOUR (INCLUDES THE OAT BRAN), MODIFIED FOOD STARCH, WHEAT STARCH, SUGAR, SALT, OAT FIBER, TRISODIUM PHOSPHATE, CALCIUM CARBONATE, VITAMIN E (MIXED TOCOPHEROLS) ADDED TO PRESERVE FRESHNESS. **VITAMINS AND MINERALS:** VITAMIN C (SODIUM ASCORBATE), IRON AND ZINC (MINERAL NUTRIENTS), A B VITAMIN (NIACIN), VITAMIN B_6 (PYRIDOXINE HYDROCHLORIDE), VITAMIN A (PALMITATE), VITAMIN B_2 (RIBOFLAVIN), VITAMIN B_1 (THIAMIN MONONITRATE), A B VITAMIN (FOLIC ACID), VITAMIN D.

1. If you choose a cereal based on nutritional value alone, which cereal would you eat (A, B, C, or D)? Give reasons for your answer.

____

____

____

____

____

2. If you were on a diet and wanted to limit your fat intake, which cereal would you choose? Why?

____

____

____

____

____

3. A = Low Fat Granola, B = Life Cereal, C = Corn Flakes, and D = Cheerios. Now that you know the identities of the cereals, would you choose the same cereal? Why or why not?

____

____

____

____

____

Activity 3.

Here are some facts about health care spending in the United States and Canada. Fill in the blanks with an appropriate modal or verb form. Use the existing modal and verb forms to help you decide whether the *if* clause results in an expected consequence in the main clause (as in sentence #1) or an imagined consequence in the main clause (as in sentence #2).

1. If the clinic *is* open, I *will* go.
2. If the clinic *were* open, I *would* go.

FOR YOUR INFORMATION In 1994, the United States was one of the few industrialized nations that did not provide universal health care to its citizens. That year the U.S. Congress debated the advantages and disadvantages of providing such care, including a compromise package that would provide 95 percent of Americans with health coverage. The Congress consists of 100 Senators in the Senate and 435 Representatives in the House of Representatives.

1. *Fact*: All U.S. government employees automatically receive health care benefits. If Congress passed health reform legislation designed to achieve 95 percent coverage, which five senators ______________ (1) go without? Paul Simon, Democratic Senator from Illinois, claimed that even Senators against universal health care to U.S. citizens "______________ (2) not vote for a law that excluded 5 percent of them."
2. *Fact*: Health care spending in the United States reached $942 billion in 1993, over 14 percent of the gross domestic product.[1] If health care spending continues at the same rate, it ______________ (3) top $1 trillion in 1994. Without reform, health care spending ______________ (4) rise to 18 percent of the gross domestic product in the year 2000.

3. If unnecessary medical tests and procedures ______(5)______ eliminated, it could save up to $130 billion a year, according to some estimates.

4. *Fact*: According to data from Health and Welfare Canada, administrative costs at Canadian hospitals average between 9 and 11 percent, compared to an average of 25 percent in the United States[2] If the United States ______(6)______ (adopt) the Canadian single-payer system, it would save about $50 billion a year in hospital expenses.

5. Even if the U.S. Congress ______(7)______ (pass) legislation with universal health care coverage, the Commerce Department predicts increased profits for health care companies. Universal coverage ______(8)______ increase access to medical care, which ______(9)______ lead to greater demand for medical equipment, drugs, and health care services.

6. According to Dr. Sidney Wolfe, Director of the Public Citizen Health Research Group, "total health spending would double by the year 2000 if it ______(10)______ (rise) at the rates foreseen by the Commerce Department."[3]

---

[1]Based on R. Pear, "$1 Trillion in Health Costs Is Predicted," *The New York Times,* Dec. 29, 1993.

[2]Based on Boston (AP), "Paperwork Is 25 Percent of Hospital Costs," *Beloit Daily News,* Aug. 6, 1993.

[3]Adapted from Robert Pear, "$1 Trillion in Health Costs Is Predicted," *The New York Times,* Dec. 29, 1993.

Activity 4

Groups. Imagine that you are a health care expert. You and other public health officials have to decide which of the following medical services you would recommend for universal health coverage in a home state, province, or country. You have a limited budget and can only include seven of the following 10 items in the health plan. Go over any vocabulary that is new to you and discuss which items you would include. Rate them from 1 to 7, where 1 = most important. Be prepared to give reasons for your choices. Then compare your choices to other groups'.

______ prenatal care

______ organ transplants (e.g., liver, kidney, heart)

______ yearly physical exams

______ dental care (excluding braces on teeth)

______ vision care (eye exams and glasses)

______ immunizations

______ injuries, serious illnesses, diseases

______ mental health care

______ home care (medical/ social services at home)

______ long-term (> 1 month) hospitalization/nursing care

Activity 5.

Read the letter and response from Dr. Gott, a U.S. physician who publishes a question and answer column on health issues. Fill in the blanks with an appropriate modal. In some cases, more than one modal is possible. Be prepared to give reasons for your answers. (The original version of this column appears at the end of this lesson.)

HERE'S A WAKE-UP CALL FOR SNORER

DEAR DR. GOTT: My husband has a snoring problem. He snores while on his back, stomach, sitting, or sometimes even driving. When he snores, he holds his breath so long that it frightens me, and he often chokes on his **saliva.** What ________ (1) I do to help him when he completely refuses to see a doctor?

DEAR READER: Except for sleeping in the guestroom, there's not much you ________ (2) do to stop your husband's snoring. However, there is much that he ________ (3) do to help himself.

If he drinks or uses prescription sleeping pills, he ________ (4) stop. These depressant drugs often make snoring worse. If he's fat, he ________ (5) lose weight. He ________ (6) see a doctor for a throat examination. As we age, the tissues of the palate, in the back of the throat, often **sag** and become **flaccid,** partially blocking the airway. Snoring, with or without apnea (stopping breathing), ________ (7) result.

If this is your husband's problem, a new form of therapy (using laser surgery) ________ (8) help him enormously. The doctor ________ (9) advise you both—but, for obvious reasons, your husband ________ (10)n't get the help he needs until he stops being so childish and seeks out the proper resources. Show him my answer to your question.

Slightly adapted from Peter H. Gott, "Dr. Gott: Here's a Wake-Up Call for Snorer," *Beloit Daily News,* July 28, 1994.

snorer a person who makes snorting noises through the mouth and nose while sleeping
saliva the liquid produced by the salivary and mucous glands in the mouth
sag fall from pressure or weight, become less firm
flaccid lacking firmness

Activity 6.

If someone is sick, at what point should he or she go to a doctor? Choose a health problem you are familiar with (e.g., headaches, ear infections, skin problems, or something else) and write up a list of symptoms (indications of the problem). Then, on a separate page, write up your recommendations on when to see a doctor. Include several sentences with *if* clauses.

Health problem ________________________________

Symptoms

1. ________________________________
2. ________________________________
3. ________________________________
4. ________________________________

Your advice (on a separate page)

HERE'S A WAKE-UP CALL FOR SNORER

by Peter H. Gott, M.D.

DEAR DR. GOTT: My husband has a snoring problem. He snores while on his back, stomach, sitting, or sometimes even driving. When he snores, he holds his breath so long that it frightens me, and he often chokes on his saliva. What *can* I do to help him when he flatly refuses to see a doctor?

DEAR READER: Short of sleeping in the guestroom, there's not much you *can* do to alleviate your husband's snoring. However, there is much that he *can* do to help himself.

If he drinks or uses prescription sleeping pills, he *should* stop. These depressant drugs often aggravate the snoring.

If he's fat, he *should* lose weight.

He *should* see a doctor for a throat examination. As we age, the tissues of the palate, in the back of the throat, often sag and become flaccid, partially blocking the airway. Snoring, with or without apnea (cessation of breathing), *will* result.

If this is your husband's problem, a new form of therapy (using laser surgery) *might* help him enormously. The doctor *can* advise you both—but, for obvious reasons, your husband *won't* get the assistance he needs until he stops being so childish and seeks out the proper resources. Show him my answer to your question.

Verbals as Objects

3

CHAPTER

Lesson 10: Verbs Followed Only by *to* + Base or *-ing*

PREVIEW

How experienced a traveler are you on the information superhighway? Circle the terms that you know or use.

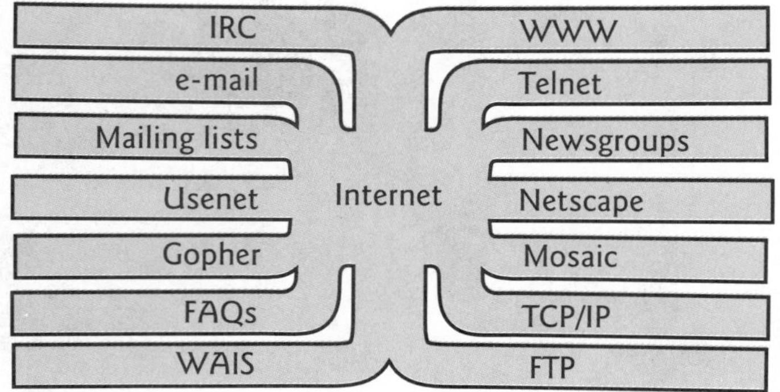

(1) If you *want* to communicate quickly with a friend or colleague at work or overseas, *try* using **e-mail**. (2) If you would *like* to keep up-to-date in a particular area, say jazz music, *consider* subscribing to a mailing list. (3) But if you *prefer* **surfing the Net** to check out what's available, you'll *need* to become familiar with WWW—World-Wide Web. (4) The Internet, a vast network of networks on which computers all over the world can communicate with one another, makes these and many other services possible.

e-mail electronic mail, communicating with others via computer
surfing the Net changing from one location to another on the Internet, like switching channels on TV

Table 3.1 lists and defines some terms related to the Internet. You will see some of these terms in this lesson.

TABLE 13.1 Some Terms Used on the Internet

TERM	MEANING
FAQs	Frequently asked questions
FTP	File Transfer Protocol—used for retrieving large documents from remote computers
Gopher	A system for moving quickly from one place to another on the Internet
IRC	Internet Relay Chat—similar to CB radio where everyone can participate in the conversation
Mailing lists	E-mail on a particular topic that subscribers can read and respond to
Mosaic + Netscape	Net browsers that allow users to find related sources of information on the World-Wide Web
Newsgroups	Electronic bulletin boards on a multitude of topics, including FAQs on those topics
Telnet	A way of logging on to computers elsewhere
TCP/IP	Transmission Control Protocol/Internet Protocol—used to directly connect to the Internet and all of its services
Usenet	A collection of electronic bulletin boards arranged by general categories and topics, for example, soc.culture.bosna.herzgvna
WAIS	Wide Area Information Servers—tools for searching huge libraries of information on the "Net" (Internet)
WWW	World-Wide Web—an information search tool that organizes its contents by subject area

In the passage in the Preview, verbs with verbals are underlined. The verbs control the form of the **verbals** that follow. Verbals are verb forms without tense. Some verbs are followed only by ***to*** **+ base** verbals (infinitives), others only by ***-ing*** verbals (gerunds), and still others, by either ***to*** **+ base** or ***-ing.***

1. In the Preview passage, there are two verbs (in italic) that can *only* be followed by a ***to*** **+ base** verbal. Can you find them?

   ____

2. There is one verb (in italic) that can *only* be followed by an ***-ing*** verbal. Can you find it?______________

3. Three verbs (in italic) are left. They can be followed by either ***to*** **+ base** or ***-ing.*** List these verbs.

   ____

PRESENTATION

Verb + Object (V O) is one of the three common predicate patterns in English.* This chapter focuses on just one of many fillers of the object position: verbal phrases in O. A **verbal phrase** refers to a verbal plus the words that follow. Together, the verb and any verbal phrase make up the **predicate** of a sentence. The following sentence shows how verbs, verbals, and the predicate relate to one another:

Predicate

You'll need **to become familiar with WWW—World-Wide Web.**

Auxiliary | Verb | Verbal | Verbal Phrase

*The two other predicate patterns are Verb + Complement and Verb + Predicate Adverbial. See *The Tapestry Grammar,* Chapter 11, for additional information.

This lesson reviews two groups of verbs: verbs that *always* take ***to*** **+ base** and verbs that *always* take ***-ing.*** Table 3.2 lists some common verbs in these two groups.

TABLE 3.2 Verbs Followed ONLY by ***to*** **+ Base** or ONLY by ***-ing*** Verbal Phrases

A. VERBS FOLLOWED BY *to* + base

Below is a list of some common verbs which **ALWAYS** take ***to*** **+ base, NEVER** the ***-ing*** form in **O.**

agree	beg	decide	endeavor	hesitate	need	prepare	refuse	seem	want
appear	claim	demand	expect	hope	neglect	pretend	resolve	swear	wish
ask	consent	deserve	fail	long	offer	promise	seek	tend	

You **want** (V) to find out how to research your family's history (O).

B. VERBS FOLLOWED BY *-ing*

Below is a list of some common verbs that **ALWAYS** take the ***-ing*** in the O), **NEVER *to* + base.**

admit (to)	consider	detest	escape	include	object to	put off	resent	teach
appreciate	defend	discuss	facilitate	keep (on)	omit	quit	resist	tolerate
avoid	delay	doubt	favor	mention	permit	recall	resume	
complete	deny	endure	finish	mind	postpone	recommend	risk	
confess (to)	despise	enjoy	give up	miss	practice	renounce	suggest	

Six of these verbs have prepositions after them. Where the preposition is printed in parentheses, it is optional. If the preposition is printed without parentheses, it must be used, as in for example put off.

You could **consider** (V) subscribing to a mailing list on genealogy (O).

LEARNING STRATEGY

Managing Your Learning: Using a dictionalry to look up a verb that is not listed in your textbook will help you enrich your vocabulary.

Many dictionaries list the form of the verbal that a verb takes. For further information about Verb + Object predicates, see *The Tapestry Grammar,* Chapter. 11, pages 265–275. See pages 276–289 for other common predicate patterns.

PRACTICE

Activity 1

What's in an e-mail address? Read the passage, "How to Be Well-Connected Electronically," and then:

1. Underline all the verbals (***to*** **+ base** or ***-ing***) in the *predicate* position. (Look for seven.)
2. After the passage, list the verbs that take **only** ***to*** **+ base** verbals and the verbs that take only ***-ing*** verbals under the two columns: Verbs + ***to*** + **base** and Verb + ***-ing.*** (Look for five.) Check a dictionary or ask a native English speaker if you need help.

Sorting Mail, Electronically

Internet mail addresses use a hierarchical system of names to make sense of the millions of computers served. The name of each computer or "domain" contains at least two words (or abbreviations) and at most five, separated by periods, with the top of the hierarchy at the right. As the number of computers on the Internet has grown, so have the methods by which the domain name system has been applied.

1 Here is the hypothetical Internet address of Beatrice Smith, vice president of personnel at Acme Incorporated.

bsmith@admin.acme.com

USER ID Identifies the personal mailbox of the user.

SUB-DOMAINS Specify the company name and divisions of the compnay.

TOP-LEVEL DOMAIN Indicates the type of organization the computer belongs to. In this case, ".com" is commercial. Other top-level domains include ".edu" (education) and ".gov" (government).

2 The hypothetical Internet address of an engineer with Network Research Belgium.

koenraad@nrb.be

USER ID

SUB-DOMAIN

TOP-LEVEL DOMAIN Each country now has its own two-letter top-level domain

Source: The New York Times, June 6, 1994. Reprinted by permission.

HOW TO BE WELL-CONNECTED ELECTRONICALLY

(1) Having an e-mail address is almost a requirement for membership in high-tech communities. (2) Not having one suggests being less than well connected, socially and technologically.

(3) How do you tell an **elite** address from a common one? (4) To find out, you need to look to the right of the @ sign in an e-mail address—to the domain at the end. (5) The domain may be broken up into one or more subdomains, each separated by periods. (6) If you enjoy impressing people, get an e-mail address that is "close to the Net." (7) It should also be one you don't have to pay for. (8) For example, Jane Doe, who works for Widget Enterprises Inc., might have the address jdoe@widget.com. (9) (The domain ".com" is an abbreviation for a commercial address.) (10) John P. Mills may have the address jpmills@aol.com, where the subdomain "aol" stands for America Online, a commercial service that offers to connect anyone to the Internet who is willing to pay a monthly fee. (11) It is not exclusive and not as "close to the Net" as Jane Doe's address, which is linked directly through her company.

(12) But the ultimate e-mail status goes to people whose domain name *is* their last name. (13) Mark Seiden, a computer consultant who has a sophisticated link to the Internet via a powerful computer, is one of the select few. (14) His address: MIS@seiden.com. (15) Seiden obviously doesn't mind receiving recognition from other Net users: "It's the ultimate **vanity license plate** in **cyberspace,"** he says.

Adapted from Steve Lohr, "Can E-Mail Cachet = jpmorgan@park.ave?," *The New York Times*, June 6, 1994.

elite a small, privileged group
vanity license plate an automobilie license plate with a combination of letters and numbers selected and purchased by the owner
cyberspace the world of communication made possible by computers

Verb + *to* + base	**Verb + *-ing***
____________________	____________________
____________________	____________________
____________________	____________________
____________________	____________________
____________________	____________________

Activity 2

Partners. Work with a partner who knows something about computers. Situation: A friend of yours wants to buy a new computer, but he doesn't know what kind to buy or how to begin. Since you've had a computer for years, you offer to help.

1. Make a list of things your friend needs to do, things he could do (but aren't essential), and things he should avoid doing to shop for a computer. Try to be as helpful as possible.
2. After you have completed your list, compare it with another pair's list. Make any changes to your lists that you think are needed.

Activity 3

Read the following passage on newsgroup etiquette ("netiquette"). You may want to review Table 3.2 first. Then, try to complete the sentences with the appropriate verbal (***to* + base** or ***-ing***) without looking at the table.

If you have just joined a newsgroup (an electronic bulletin board), we recommend ________________ (1) (follow) these guidelines:

1. To understand how newsgroup members communicate, expect ________________ (2) (spend) a couple of weeks just reading messages before you post your own.
2. Resolve ________________ (3) (keep) your messages brief and to the point.
3. Avoid ________________ (4) (get) off the topic of your newsgroup.
4. If you're responding to a message, be prepared ________________ (5) (summarize or quote) relevant parts of the message for others who may have missed it.
5. Don't risk ________________ (6) (write) flames (angry e-mail messages) unless you can take the heat.
6. Refuse ________________ (7) (publish) private messages without permission.
7. Resist ________________ (8) (type) in all capital letters. (It sounds like YOU'RE SHOUTING.)
8. Promise not ________________ (9) (flame) people for bad grammar or spelling errors. (E-mail users often type quickly without editing their messages.)
9. Resolve not ________________ (10) (send) unwanted advertisements via e-mail.

Adapted from "FAQs (Frequently Asked Questions)," *Time,* July 25, 1994.

Activity 4

You manage a bookstore with a resource section on computers and software. Read the book advertisements on the next page and respond to the following situations by writing a brief note or a dialogue. Be creative in your responses. Whenever possible, use verbs that require a ***to* + base** or an ***-ing*** verbal in your answers.

Internet and Online Resources

What's On The Internet? • Eric Gagnon (1994) • $19.95 (pb) • 262 pages • #B180P This book is distinct from other online books in that it focuses entirely on the Internet and its most popular areas, it targets primarily a non-technical audience, and it offers a ready reference for finding newsgroups by topic. Also contains a coupon for a free (with $5 for shipping) Mac/PC disk for easily finding groups by keyword.

Internet Starter Kit For Windows • Adam C. Engst (1994) • $29.95 (pb) • 656 pages #B176P • For readers who want to get on the Internet but don't know where to start, this is the source of all information. This large volume explains how to get connected, where to look for what, and how to master e-mail, downloading, ftp sites, and more—everything readers need to navigate this huge network. Includes a disk for getting online and using the Internet; two weeks free connect time with full Internet access; and covers newsgroups, e-mail, Internet resources, usenet, UUCP access, and more.

A Must Read

Education on the Internet: A Hands-on Book of Ideas, Resources, Projects, and Advice • Jill H. Ellsworth (1994) • $25.00 (pb) • 591 pages • #B178P • Find out how to use the Internet for learning, teaching or research. Discover hundreds of education-oriented mailing lists, newsgroups, databases, and other resources. Offers ideas and projects for everyone—from kindergartners to grad students, from classroom teachers to university professors.

Video

Information Superhighway: Understanding and Using the Internet — A Step-By-Step Guide • $29.95 • 30 minutes VHS • #V104 • Featuring easy-to-use Windows Internet access application, the "Information Superhighway" video will show you a high-quality presentation of the basic protocols of e-mail, file transfer protocol and telnet as well as the latest Internet tools such as gopher, world wide web, archie, veronica and WAIS. Designed with the novice PC user in mind, this tutorial is both fun and interesting.

New Rider's Official Internet Yellow Pages • Christine Maxwell, et al (1994) $29.95 (pb) • 800 pages • #B181P • Finally there's a reference to the Internet as easy to use as a phone book. From acting to zoology, users can look up their favorite topics and discover how to use the Internet to learn more. Perfect for educators, professionals, researchers and other Internet explorers. Provides up-to-date listings, addresses, and descriptions of Internet services that no one else has.

The Complete Idiot's Guide to The Internet • Peter Kent (1994) • $19.95 (pb) 400 pages • #B177P • This lighthearted but information-packed guide helps newcomers hook up to—and find their way around—this sprawling network. The guide comes with a disk packed with free software programs, and contains everything reluctant users could possibly need to access the Internet.

Little Online Book: A Gentle Introduction to Modems, Online Services, Electronic Bulletin Boards, and the Internet • Alfred Glossbrenner (1994) • $17.95 (pb) • 400 pages • #B179P This book assumes you know absolutely nothing about online communications. Written in a relaxed, conversational style, this book covers the following topics: choosing a modem that's right for you; getting online for free; basic features of America Online, CompuServe, Delphi, GEnie, and Prodigy; and the six main functions of the Internet: e-mail, UseNet newsgroups, mailing lists, files, Internet relay chat, and telnet.

The Children's Machine—Rethinking Schools in the Age of the Computer Seymour Papert (1993) • $12.00 (pb) • 242 pages • #B172P • In his classic book, *Mindstorms: Children, Computers, and Powerful Ideas*, Seymour Papert set out a vision of how computers could change schools. In *The Children's Machine* he now looks back over a decade during which American schools acquired more than three million computers and assesses progress and resistance to progress.

Source: Teacher Magazine, March 1995, p. 39. Reprinted by permission.

1. A customer who has a computer at home would like to use e-mail for the first time. Which book(s) would you recommend? Why?
2. An elementary school teacher would like some information about how to find information useful for himself and his students on the Internet. Which book(s) does he need to read? Why?
3. A customer wants to get an Internet resource book for his mother-in-law, who is interested in doing genealogy research via computer. She plans to use a commercial online service, such as SeniorNet (part of America Online). Which book(s) would you suggest reading?
4. A customer enters the bookstore looking for a how-to manual on the Internet. She tells you she has a hard time reading manuals of any kind because she learns best by watching and doing. Which book(s) or other materials should she consider buying?

Activity 5

Partners/Groups. With a partner, rewrite one of your responses in Activity 4 as a dialogue. (If you wrote a dialogue, read it over with a partner and make any changes you think are necessary.) Practice your dialogue together and perform it for your group or class.

Lesson 11: Verbs Followed by *to* + Base or by *-ing*

PREVIEW

Fact or fiction? Do you think the following activities occur in real life? Check the appropriate column.

	Yes	No	Maybe
1. People buy police scanners to listen to private conversations over cellular and cordless phones.	_____	_____	_____
2. Employers quietly check employees' electronic mail without their knowledge.	_____	_____	_____
3. The Post Office sells its change-of-address lists to private mail-order companies.	_____	_____	_____
4. Private investigators use motor vehicle records to find out the addresses of people their clients wish to contact.	_____	_____	_____
5. Credit bureaus sell credit reports on someone else without checking the requester's identity.	_____	_____	_____

If you answered "yes" to all five, you're right. Although most employers don't **try** to invade people's privacy, it has happened. But as Janlori Goldman, head of the Privacy and Technology Project of the American Civil Liberties Union,* points out, they don't **try** to protect personal privacy either.

*A U.S. organization that strongly believes in and lobbies for the protection of civil rights, such as freedom of speech.

In the above paragraph, the verb *try* is followed by a ***to* + base** verbal (underlined). However *try* can be followed by ***to* + base** or by ***-ing.*** In other words, both of the following are possible:

- They tried to protect personal privacy.
- They tried protecting personal privacy.

The different verbals in the two sentences signal a difference in meaning. In the first sentence, the action was begun but was not completed. In the second one, the action was completed but was not successful.

PRESENTATION

Try is one of several verbs that can be followed by ***to* + base** or by ***-ing.*** Table 3.3 lists common verbs that follow this pattern.

Most verbs in Table 3.3 do *not* change the meaning of a sentence when they are followed by ***to* + base** or ***-ing.*** For example, the following two sentences mean the same:

- She likes to use e-mail.
- She likes using e-mail.

However, with a few verbs, such as "stop," "try," "remember," or "forget," the form of the verbal *does* change the meaning:

- Rosa stopped to answer the phone. (She stopped first, then answered the phone.)
- Rosa stopped answering the phone. (She finished answering the phone first, then did not answer any more calls.)

TABLE 3.3 Verbs Followed by either ***to*** **+ base** or ***-ing*** Verbal Phrases

attempt	decline	intend	regret
(can't) bear	deserve	learn	remember
begin	dread	like	(can't) stand
cease	fear	love	start
choose	forget	mean	stop
commence	hate	prefer	try
continue	help	propose	

In the first sentence, the action described in the verbal phrase is not yet done; in the second one, the action in the verbal phrase was completed before the action in the verb.

LEARNING STRATEGY

Remembering New Material: Making up sentences with different verbs can help you learn basic predicate patterns.

PRACTICE

Activity 1

In the following pairs of sentences, the ***to*** **+ base** and ***-ing*** verbals can change meaning. Read the sentences and answer the questions that follow:

1. **a.** Rosa **didn't remember** to unplug her computer.
   b. Rosa **didn't remember** unplugging her computer.

   There was an electrical storm that night, and Rosa's computer was damaged. In which case, (a) or (b), was Rosa sorry? How did you decide?

   ____

2. **a.** The next day Rosa **tried** to call the computer repair service, but the line was busy.
   b. The next day Rosa **tried** calling the computer repair service, but no one could help her.

   In which case, (a) or (b), did Rosa talk to someone from the repair service? ________

3. **a.** John Mills **forgot** to have his subscription to America Online (a commercial provider of network services) renewed.
   b. John Mills **forgot** having renewed his subscription to America Online and worried that AOL would disconnect his e-mail.
   The next week, when he tried to access e-mail, he got this message: THANK YOU for your subscription renewal.

   In which case, (a) or (b), did John pay his bill? ________

4. **a.** John **stopped** to check the spelling in his e-mail message.
   b. John **stopped** checking the spelling in his e-mail message.

   In which case did John decide not to check his spelling anymore? ________

   In which case did he decide to check his spelling? ________

Activity 2

Individuals/partners. Write pairs of sentences with each of the following verbs: "stop," "remember," "forget," and "try," using a ***to*** **+ base** and ***-ing*** verbal in each pair. The sentences in each pair should be different in meaning. Exchange your sentences with a partner. Try to explain the different meaning of each pair of your partner's sentences to your partner. You may need to add an additional phrase or sentence for the contrast in meaning to be clear (as in Activity 1).

Activity 3

Read the information about a new telephone service available to customers. You may wish to review Table 3.3 before you answer the questions that follow.

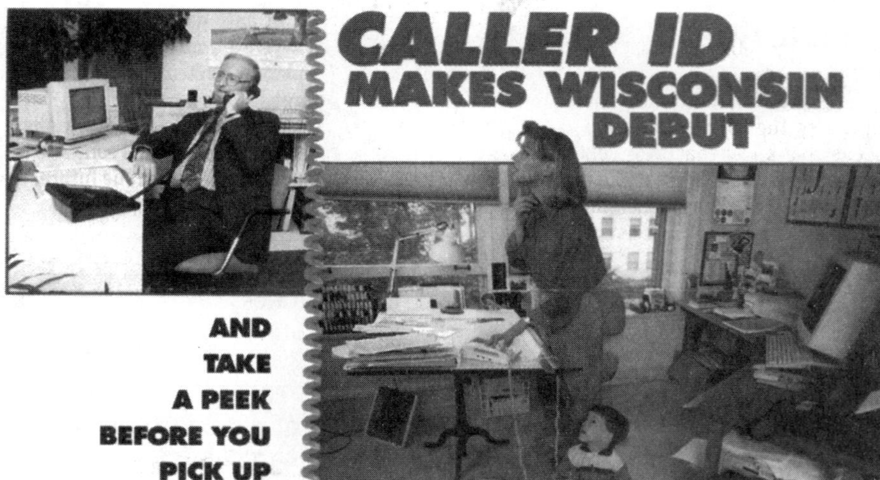

Now is a great time to simplify your life. The convenience, control and privacy of Caller ID* is now available in Wisconsin. And for a limited time, Ameritech is offering Caller ID at impressive savings.

Caller ID makes life easier in your home by letting you know who's calling before you answer the phone. It also provides you with a record of calls (up to 60), even if callers hang up without leaving a message. That means you have the convenience of being able to prepare for a caller, control over who should answer the call, the privacy of prioritizing incoming calls, and the ability to identify missed calls.

Caller ID service provides solutions for a variety of different lifestyles. For instance, if you work at home, you're able to recognize a business call from a personal call, letting you answer business calls properly or prepare whatever information you'll need for a smooth conversation. If you're working on a tight deadline, you can choose to answer the urgent calls, and let the others go to Voice Mail or an answering machine.

In a busy household, you can use Caller ID to distinguish whom a call is for so you don't have to play receptionist for your kids. And having a stored list of callers lets you return calls even if the kids lose a message or forget to take down a number.

Order Caller ID now, and you'll receive free installation and a free 30-day trial of the Caller ID display unit. This new, full-function display unit can be shipped to your door and can be paid through installment billing on your phone bill.

Call your friendly Ameritech service representative today at 1-800-AROUND U and order the convenience of Caller ID.

* Services may not be available in all areas. Both parties must be in specially equipped areas for Caller ID to work.
Callers are able to block the Caller ID display of their phone number by dialing *67 (or 1-1-6-7 on a rotary phone) prior to placing the call. A stuttered confirmation tone, followed by a dial tone, confirms that blocking is activated.

Source: Ameritech. Reprinted by permission.

1. There is one verb in the advertisment in paragraph 3 that can take either a ***to* + base** or an ***-ing*** verbal. What is it? ____________

2. Answer the following questions, using either a ***to* + base** or an ***-ing*** verbal. If the form of the verbal changes the meaning, circle the verb in your sentence.

   a. When could customers begin using Caller ID?

   ____

   b. Why might customers choose to order Caller ID?

   ____

   c. Why might other customers prefer *not* to get Caller ID?

   ____

   d. Why might some Wisconsin residents try to block Caller ID? (Read the small print on the Ameritech ad.)

   ____

Activity 4

Imagine that you live in a metropolitan area that has Caller ID. Would you like to have this service? Write a paragraph explaining why you would or would not like to have Caller ID. Try to use several verbs from Tables 3.2 and 3.3.

Activity 5

Read the passage about the electronic transfer of public records. Then answer the question that follows.

PUBLIC RECORDS GO PUBLIC

(1) A growing number of **firms** buy and sell public records electronically for a **fee**. (2) Prentice-Hall Online, based in Irvine, California, has **accessed** 300 million public records in 45 states. (3) To find out what kind of information Prentice-Hall Online collects, Dr. Peter Tippett, manager of data security for a software company in Washington, typed in his own name. (4) He found the following records related to his professional and private life: a copy of his medical license (he's also an emergency room physician), the price he paid for his house, the number of bathrooms it has, the size of his front yard, former addresses, and the median income for households in his neighborhood. (5) This information is used by those who want to **market** certain products, locate missing individuals, find out the value of real estate, and estimate the personal assets of individuals, among other things.

(6) "Instead of having to physically go to a public building, look someone in the eye, and ask for information, you can get it all with one command on the computer, which makes it too easy," said Tippet, who is also a board member of the Computer Ethics Institute, a non-profit research group. (7) Still, as Jeffrey Alperin, a vice president of Information America, Inc., says, "This is not **sneaky** stuff; it's all publicly available information." (8) If you would like to find out how public this information is, Prentice-Hall charges $150 to sign up for Online and has a minimum monthly charge of $100.

Adapted from Shelley Emling, "Public Record Now Online via Prentice-Hall," *Saint Paul Pioneer Press,* Aug. 14, 1994.

firms businesses
fee money charged for a service or product
access obtain
market sell for a fee
sneaky acquired in secret, not obtained openly

How public should public records be? Germany has strict regulations against electronic invasions of privacy; the United States has almost none. Think about motor vehicle records, criminal records, home mortgage records, subscriptions to newspapers and magazines, and tax records. Take a position on the question and support it in about a page. Try to use some verbs from Table 3.3.

Lesson 12: Verbs Followed by "Subject" Plus Verbal Phrase

PREVIEW

FUGITIVE SOUGHT

(1) Looking for criminals has become a high-tech **enterprise**. (2) But there is a right way and a wrong way to do it on the Internet. (3) In late June and early July 1994, Special Agent Jim Christy, director of the Air Force computer crimes investigation division, tried to locate an Air Force computer technician who was suspected of murdering his wife and two children with a **machete** in Florida. (4) The man, Edward Zakrzewski, regularly communicated via Internet to people all over the world. (5) Christy posted a message called Fugitive Sought to more than 14,000 newsgroups on the Internet. (6) He invited users to contact him if they knew anything about where Zakrzewski was. (7) Receiving an **unsolicited** message was bad enough for many people, but the real problem was that the message included many pages of unreadable computer symbols that took people five to 10 minutes to page through. (8) The multiple pages were really a digitalized "wanted" poster for Zakrzewski and the numbers of some agencies to contact. (9) But most people didn't know that, or if they did, they didn't have the software to decode the symbols into a picture of Zakrzewski.

Based on Tod Copilevitz [*Dallas Morning News*], "Air Force's Tracking of Fugitive in Cyberspace Irks Some," *Saint Paul Pioneer Press,* Aug. 14, 1994.

fugitive a person who runs away from the police
enterprise business
machete a large heavy knife used for cutting vegetation and as a weapon
unsolicited not asked for

Like sending messages electronically, using the right verbal patterns can get complicated. In Lessons 10 and 11 we introduced two patterns: (1) verbs that take ONLY ***to* + base** or ***-ing;*** and (2) verbs that take EITHER ***to* + base** OR ***-ing.*** Lesson 12 practices a third pattern: verbs that are followed by a "subject" plus a verbal phrase. There is an example of the third pattern in sentence (6) in the text you just read. What "subject" and type of verbal (***to* + base** or ***-ing***) follows the verb?

PRESENTATION

The pattern **"subject" + verbal phrase** occurs after three main groups of verbs: verbs of permission or intention, verbs of perception, and verbs of emotion. Table 3.4 lists common verbs in each of these three groups.

TABLE 3.4 Verbs Followed by "Subject" + Verbal Phrases

VERBS OF PERMISSION OR INTENTION—GROUP I				
allow authorize compel	expect force get	invite mean permit	persuade teach tell	train wish
VERBS OF PERMISSION OR INTENTION—GROUP 2				
advise agree (for)* arrange (for)* ask (for)	beg (for) command desire (for) instruct	intend (for) order pray (for)* prefer (for)	propose recommend request (for) require	stipulate (for)* urge vote (for)* want
VERBS OF PERCEPTION				
feel hear	notice observe	overhear see	smell watch	
VERBS OF EMOTION				
detest dislike dread forget	imagine involve justify (don't) mind	miss recall regret relish	remember resent risk (can't) stand	

*_For_ is required after the verb with this pattern. For example, We **arranged for** him to go.

Verbs of permission or intention. Verbs of permission or intention can be divided into two subgroups:

1. Subgroup 1: Uses object form of pronoun[1] as **"subject" + _to_ + base verbal**:
   - Special Agent Christy's superiors authorized **him** to post a message on the Internet.
2. Subgroup 2.
   a. Basic pattern: Uses object pronoun as **"subject" + _to_ + base verbal.** Some of these verbs *may* be followed by **for** before the "subject" and others *must* be followed by **for:**
      - Special Agent Christy asked (for) **people** to contact him if they had any relevant information. (**for** optional)
      - He arranged for **them** to have the appropriate phone numbers and e-mail addresses. (**for** required)

   b. Additional pattern: Uses *that* + the subject form of the pronoun + base form of verb. A few verbs (instruct, want) do not allow this additional pattern:[2]
      - Christy asked that **people** contact him—and they did.

[1]Pronouns *or* noun phrases can occur as "subjects." If a pronoun is the "subject," it occurs in the object form: "me," "you," "him," "her," "it," "us," "them."

[2]There may be some difference between British and American speakers of English here.

Verbs of perception. These verbs take the object form of the pronoun as **"subject" + the base form** or ***-ing:***

- Christy heard **people** *become* angry about the long, mostly unreadable e-mail message he had sent.
- Christy heard **them** *becoming* angry about the e-mail message he had sent.

IT WORKS! Learning Strategy: Using Different Verb Patterns

Verbs of emotion. These verbs take *either* the object form *or* the possessive form of the pronoun as "subject." They are only followed by an *-ing* verbal:

- Users resented **him** using the Internet to send an unsolicited message to thousands. (object pronoun)
- Users resented **his** using the Internet to send an unsolicited message to thousands. (possessive)

The two sentences mean the same, but the use of the possessive in the second sentence is more formal. Table 3.5 summarizes the different patterns of verbal phrases in the object position (O) from Lessons 10–12.

TABLE 3.5 Summary of Verb + Verbal Phrase Patterns

VERBS FOLLOWED BY *to* + base ONLY

agree	beg	decide	endeavor	hesitate	need	prepare	refuse	seem	want
appear	claim	demand	expect	hope	neglect	pretend	resolve	swear	wish
ask	consent	deserve	fail	long	offer	promise	seek	tend	

VERBS FOLLOWED BY *-ing* ONLY

admit (to)	consider	detest	escape	include	object to	put off	resent	teach
appreciate	defend	discuss	facilitate	keep (on)	omit	quit	resist	tolerate
avoid	delay	doubt	favor	mention	permit	recall	resume	
complete	deny	endure	finish	mind	postpone	recommend	risk	
confess (to)	despise	enjoy	give up	miss	practice	renounce	suggest	

VERBS FOLLOWED BY *to* + base OR *-ing*

attempt	cease	continue	dread	hate	learn	mean	regret	start
(can't) bear	choose	decline	fear	help	like	prefer	remember	stop
begin	commence	deserve	forget	intend	love	propose	(can't) stand	try

VERBS FOLLOWED BY "Subject" + VERBAL PHRASES

Verbs of permission or intention

Group 1

allow	compel	force	invite	permit	teach	train
authorize	expect	get	mean	persuade	tell	wish

Group 2

advise	ask (for)	desire (for)	order	propose	require	vote (for)*
agree (for)*	beg (for)	instruct	pray (for)*	recommend	stipulate (for)*	want
arrange (for)*	command	intend (for)	prefer (for)	request (for)	urge	

Verbs of perception

feel	hear	notice	observe	overhear	see	smell	watch

Verbs of emotion

detest	dread	imagine	justify	miss	regret	remember	risk
dislike	forget	involve	(don't) mind	recall	relish	resent	(can't) stand

**For* is required after the verb.

PRACTICE

Activity 1
What do you think?

1. Do men or women use the Internet more? ______________________
2. Which age group uses the Internet the most? (a) 16–20, (b) 21–25, (c) 26–30, (d) 31–35, (e) 36–40, (f) 41–50, or (g) over 50? ______

Here are some facts about the age and gender of Internet users:

Male	Female
95 percent	5 percent

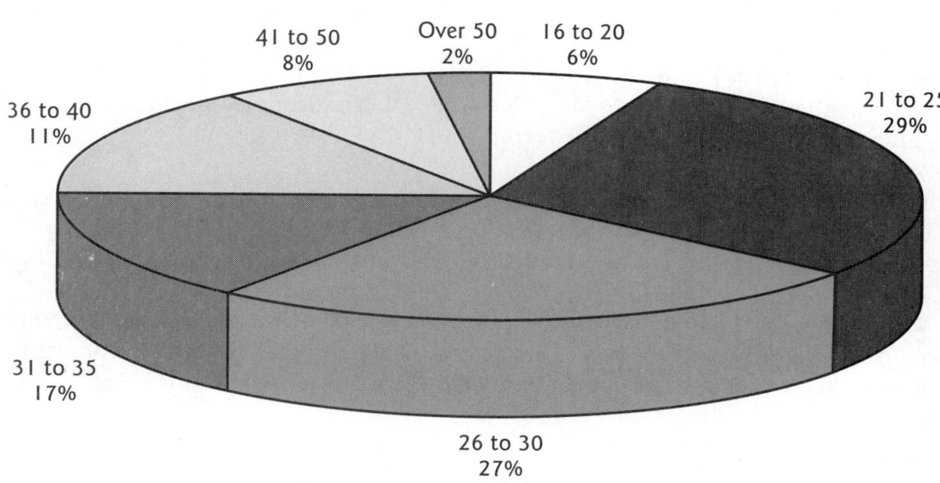

Internet Users by Age.

Were you surprised by any of the facts? Answer the following questions, using verbs that take the **"subject" + verbal phrase** pattern as much as possible:

1. What age group did you expect to use the Internet the most?
I expected 16- to 20-year-olds to use the Internet the most.
____
2. Have you observed anyone over 50 using the Internet (including e-mail)? ________
____
3. Have you overheard any women talk about the Internet (including e-mail)? ________
____
4. Can you imagine more women using the Internet in the future? Why or why not?
____
____
5. Would you urge any age group to use the Internet more? Why or why not? ________
____
____

Activity 2

Individuals/partners. Imagine that you are a marketing specialist for one of the commercial online providers, such as America Online®, CompuServe®, Delphi®, or Prodigy®.

You know that women and certain age groups make up only a small proportion of Internet users. Your job is to increase those proportions. Choose (1) or (2) to complete. Try to use verbs from Table 3.5 whenever you can:

1. Write a short memo to your boss, the Vice-President of Marketing. In the memo, list the strategies you propose to increase the proportion of women and other age group subscribers to your company. (Remember that you're really doing two things here: (1) trying to attract new users to the Internet; and (2) trying to attract new subscribers to *your* company.) You may find phrases such as the following helpful:

   I agree that
   I propose that
   I recommend that
   I request that
   I noticed [someone] + base/base + *-ing*
   I observed [someone] + base/base + *-ing*
   First, second, third, finally,
   To begin with, next, then, lastly,
   Most importantly, equally important, also important,

   I expect [someone] *to* + base
   I urge [someone] *to* + base
   I recommend [someone] *to* + base
   I can justify [someone] base + *-ing*

2. Write a short dialogue between you (a market specialist for one of the commercial online providers) and your boss. Describe your plan for increasing the proportion of women and other age groups among your company's users. Some of the phrases listed in (1) may be helpful to you.

Activity 3

Increasing numbers of older users (those over 55) *are* beginning to use the Internet. Many are using commercial computer services specially designed for seniors, such as America Online's SeniorNet, Delphi's Senior Forum, and Prodigy's Senior BB (bulletin board). Read one senior's story about using the Internet. Then respond to one or more of the questions that follow in about a paragraph.

At 5:30 A.M. in Bloomfield Township, Michigan, 67-year-old Mimi Connelly gets up and goes directly to her cyberspace station: a Macintosh computer. She has a handful of projects in progress—and she has transferred nearly all of them online. Connelly, a master gardener, is helping start up a **green-thumb** group on the Greater Detroit Free-Net, a free community-wide system. She receives and sends e-mail to new friends she has met in cyberspace as well as old friends she has convinced to join a computer service. Her favorite mail, however, comes from her four sons who are also **online.** Now she is teaching her husband, a retired Cadillac executive, how to use the Internet.

Seniors are joining the electronic world for diverse reasons—from the 70-year-old on Prodigy who has passed on memories of two-potato stew during the Great Depression for a college student writing a paper, to the 80-year-old in CompuServe's health forum who has shared how he has managed on a new drug with fellow prostate cancer patients.

"Face it," says Roberta Paul, who helps run Prodigy's senior bulletin board from her computer in Amityville, New York, "as we grow older, we begin to lose the friends and family members we've had through the years. This is a way to have a community without uprooting yourself—or even having to leave your living room."

Adapted from Antoinette Martin, "Ultramodern Maturity," *Saint Paul Pioneer Press,* Aug. 14, 1994.

green thumb people interested in gardening
online connected to the Internet

Think of the adults in your life, especially older adults. Then choose one or more of the following questions and respond to each briefly. Try to use some verbs from Table 3.5.

1. If one or more of the older adults in your life had a computer with access to the Internet, would you encourage one to join a newsgroup (a discussion group on a particular topic)? Why or why not?
2. If you are an e-mail user, could you teach someone else to use it? For example, would you be willing to teach a parent to use e-mail?
3. Do you think knowledge of computers should be required for getting an office (or other white-collar) job?
4. If your boss required you to get Caller ID at work and then monitored your calls there, would you resent him or her doing that? Why or why not?

Activity 4

The information superhighway means high-tech consumerism—500 TV channels, home shopping, movies on demand, take-out food from fast-food chains, and multimedia game playing—to some. But to others, it "will connect people with each other, one-to-one and one-to-many, and allow them to communicate in new ways." Read the following passage about one potential use, greater access to governmental information. Fill in the blanks with an appropriate form of a verbal **(*to* + base, *-ing,*** *or* **"subject" + verbal).**

It's an election year and Vinh Truong is trying ____________1____________ (decide) whom to vote for in Congress. He recently became an American citizen and is looking forward to voting in his new country. But he's a bit confused by all the campaign ads and literature he's seen. The campaigns seem overly centered on the personalities of the candidates. He thinks it would be more helpful if they would talk about what the candidates have done and plan ________2________ (do). As a new citizen, he wants ____________3____________ (vote) responsibly, so he doesn't want ____________4____________ (rely) only on the TV ads and **flyers** that fill his mailbox.

One candidate is the **incumbent,** so Vinh wants ____________5____________ (see) how he's voted on issues Vinh cares about, such as the environment and immigration policy. His brother and sister-in-law, who live nearby, have an OmniPhone, which has a touch-display and lets them connect to information services. They told him that the voting records of local representatives are accessible for free as part of the basic package of services, and invited ____________6____________ (come over) and use their device. When Vinh arrives, his brother takes his coat and shows him to the family room, where the OmniPhone is.

His brother sits in front of the unit and taps keys for a few seconds. "OK, I've got you into the congressional voting records, but I've never used this service, so you'll have ____________7____________ (figure out) the rest on your own." Vinh sits down and looks at the screen. He sees a form with the **fields** "Name," "District," "From date," "To date," **"Bill #,"** and "Keywords." Vinh uses a data base system at work, so he is pretty sure what to do. He fills in the incumbent's name, a "From date" of two years ago, and leaves the "To date" blank to indicate the present. He types "Environment" into the "Keywords" field and punches the Search key. After a few seconds, the data base displays the message "42 bills found" and a list of bills, indicating how the congressman voted on each. Vinh scans the list, asking for more detail on some of the bills. He then changes the "keywords" field to "immigration" and repeats the process. He is pretty sure now that this congressman is not someone he wants ________________ (8) (vote for), but that depends on whether the other candidate, who hasn't held office before, is worse. While he is thinking about how to get some useful information about her, his nephew Sammy returns and says, "Are you almost done, Uncle Vinh?" "It's all yours," Vinh says, and gets up ________________ (9) (ask) his brother about the other candidate.

J. Johnson, Scenarios of people using the NII
[National Information Infrastructure].
The CPSR Newsletter, 12 (4), fall 1994.

flyer a one-page advertisement for political candidates
incumbent an elected official who is running to renew his or her term in office
field choice
bill proposed laws

Activity 5

Partners or groups. As a recent CBS news report on the Internet points out, "Nobody owns it, nobody controls it, nobody can pull the plug" (CBS News, Oct. 21, 1994). The big questions about the future of the Internet have to do with *who* gets to say *what when*. Should there be any controls on who has access or what messages are available on the Internet? Discuss your ideas with a partner or a group. Think about the conflicting interests referred to in For Your Information. Try to use some verbs from Table 3.5 in your discussion. Write up a summary of your discussion in about a page. After you finish writing, review your summary for the way it represents everyone's ideas and for the use of verbals.

FOR YOUR INFORMATION The Internet was developed as a way to communicate quickly and freely between U.S. government agencies, university researchers, and the military. It was built on the principle of universal access for all users, a principle related to the first amendment to the U.S. Constitution, which guarantees the right to free speech. Now that access to the Internet has become widely available to users of all ages, there have been questions about controlling access to information. Some people are especially concerned about children's access to pornographic and other adult materials. It is becoming increasingly important for children to become computer literate, but can we protect children and free speech at the same time? (As an indicator of society's concerns about the Internet, see the cover story in *Time* magazine's July 3, 1995 issue, "Pornography on the Internet.")

Nouns and Noun Phrases

Lesson 13: An Overview

Simple and Expanded Noun Phrases

PREVIEW

Staying single is becoming more popular—or is it? Test your knowledge. Circle your answers to the following questions. (It's okay to guess.)

1. Which country had the largest percentage of single people in 1970/1971?

   Canada Hungary Norway United States

   In 1988[1]?

   Canada Hungary Norway United States

2. Which country had the largest percentage of married people in 1970/1971?

   Canada Hungary Norway United States

   In 1988?

   Canada Hungary Norway United States

3. Which country had the largest decrease in the percentage of married people between 1970 and 1988?

   Canada Hungary Norway United States

4. What group(s) of people does the word single include?

   Never married Widowed Divorced

5. What group(s) of people does the word married include?

   Married Separated Widowed Divorced

Now look at Table 4.1 and compare your answers to the answers from the table. The numbers and percentages in the table are taken from **censuses,** official counts of a country's population.

TABLE 4.1 Population by Marital Status in Selected Countries

COUNTRY	POPULATION (15+ years)	PERCENTAGE SINGLE (Never married)	PERCENTAGE MARRIED (Married + Separated)
Canada			
1971	15,187,415	28.3	64.4
1988	20,456,000	27.4	61.9
Hungary			
1970	8,145,592	20.8	66.7
1988	8,378,461	19.5	62.6
Norway			
1970	2,938,093	27.4	63.3
1988	3,394,703	31.5	55.4
United States			
1970	145,210,098	23.4	65.2
1988	177,677,000[2]	21.9	62.7

[1]The most recent year for which comparable data are available from the United Nations, *1990 Demographic Yearbook,* New York: United Nations, 1992.

[2]Population 18 years and older.

Answers

1. The largest percentage of single people: 1970–1971: Canada
   1988: Norway
2. The largest percentage of married people: 1970–1971: Hungary
   1988: United States
3. The largest decrease in the percentage of married people (1970–1988): Norway (–7.9 percent)
4. Single refers to the group "Never married."
5. Married refers to the groups "Married" and "Separated."

Thinking about the answers

1. How similar were your answers to the ones just listed?
2. Can you think of any reasons why the percentage of married people has decreased from 1970/1971 to 1988 in all four countries?

The underlined words in the answers are all **noun phrases.** A **noun phrase** refers to a **noun** and all of its modifiers. The underlined words in answers (4) and (5) are **simple noun phrases.** The underlined words in (1) and (3) are **expanded noun phrases.** Can you explain the difference between simple and expanded noun phrases? These two terms are defined in the next section.

PRESENTATION

Positions of noun phrases. A **noun phrase** and its modifiers can be divided into four positions. Table 4.2 gives examples of words that fill each position.

TABLE 4.2 Positions of Noun Phrases

1 DETERMINER →	2 PREMODIFIER →	3 NOUN ★[1]	4 POSTMODIFIER ←
1. 0[2]		China	
2. These two		statistics	
3. Its	very large	population and size	
4. Their many	social welfare	agencies	
5. The	most common	definition	of *single* used by census takers
6. A	young	person	who is less than 15 years old

[1]The star represents the core noun of a sentence.
[2]0 refers to zero article (no article).

A **simple noun phrase** fills only two of these positions, the **determiner** and **noun** positions, as in examples (1) and (2) of Table 4.2. An **expanded noun phrase** fills the **premodifier** and/or the **postmodifier** positions in addition to the **determiner** and **noun** positions, as in examples (3) through (6) of the table. The star (★) identifies the **core noun** of a phrase or a sentence. Core nouns are important to identify because when they occur in the subject position, they agree with the main verb of a sentence.

EXAMPLE The population of many countries is increasing rapidly.
★ (population) ⟶ is

Types of nouns. Nouns fill the most important position in noun phrases. There are at least six ways to classify nouns:

	Example
1. regular and irregular plural forms	year/years; child/children
2. countable and uncountable nouns	a study/a few studies; some research [uncountable]
3. collective nouns	The majority {**agree** / **agrees**} with the mayor.
4. coordinate core nouns	People's health and education are related.
5. adjectives used as nouns	the elderly = old people
6. common nouns and proper nouns	capital cities: Manila, Ankara, Tokyo.

LEARNING STRATEGY

Managing Your Learning: Understanding certain grammatical distinctions will help you choose the right word forms.

If you are familiar with these types of nouns, skip to the Practice section in this lesson or to Lesson 14. If you would like more information, please see *The Tapestry Grammar,* Chapter 5, pages 88–93.

PRACTICE

Activity 1

Individuals/Partners. Different kinds of words can fill the four positions of noun phrases. Look over Table 4.3 and identify the different kinds of words in each of the four positions. Then check your answers with the ones that follow.

TABLE 4.3 Positions of Noun Phrases

1 DETERMINER →	2 PREMODIFIER →	3 NOUN ★[1]	4 POSTMODIFIER ←
1. 0[2]		China	
2. These two		statistics	
3. Its	very large	population and size	
4. Their many	social welfare	agencies	
5. The	most common	definition	of *single* used by census takers
6. A	young	person	who is less than 15 years old

[1]The star represents the core noun of a sentence.
[2]0 refers to zero article (no article).

What kinds of words fill these positions?

1. The **determiner** position:
   - **a.** (the, a, 0) ______________________
   - **b.** (its, their) ______________________
   - **c.** (these) ______________________
   - **d.** (many) ______________________
   - **e.** (two) ______________________
2. The **premodifier** position:
   - **a.** (large, social, most common, young) ______________________
   - **b.** (very) ______________________
   - **c.** (welfare) ______________________

3. The **core noun** position:

   a. (China, statistics, agencies, definition, person) ______________________

   b. (population and size) ______________________

4. The **postmodifier** position:

   a. (of single, by census takers) ______________________

   b. (used by census takers) ______________________

   c. (who is less than 15 years old) ______________________

Answers

1. Fillers of the **determiner** position:
   - **a.** articles
   - **b.** possessives
   - **c.** demonstratives
   - **d.** quantifiers (indefinite)
   - **e.** quantifiers (definite [numbers])
2. Fillers of the **premodifier** position:
   - **a.** adjectives
   - **b.** qualifiers (intensifiers; occur with an adjective)
   - **c.** nouns (that modify other nouns)
3. Fillers of the **core noun** position:
   - **a.** single words
   - **b.** two or more core nouns (coordinated core nouns)
4. Fillers of the **postmodifier** position:
   - **a.** Prepositional phrases
   - **b.** Verbal phrases
   - **c.** *Wh*-clauses

To review these types of words in noun phrases, see *The Tapestry Grammar*, Chapters 5 and 6.

Activity 2

Read the following excerpt on differences in women's and men's marriage patterns. Put a star (★) under the core noun of the underlined noun phrases in the subject position of the following sentences. Use arrows pointing toward the core noun (⟶) under the premodifiers and arrows pointing back to the core noun (⟵) under the postmodifiers in noun phrases. The first two sentences are done for you. If you have trouble identifying the core noun in the subject position, check the verb that follows. Is it singular or plural? This will help you find the core noun.

(1) Women in many developing areas marry when they are very young. (2) Almost 50 percent of African women, 40 percent of Asian women, and 30 percent of Latin American women are married by the age of 18. (3) Men tend to marry at older ages.(4) In Bangladesh and the Sudan, men entering their first marriage are on average more than seven years older than women marrying for the first time; in Colombia and Cuba, they are four years older. (5) Most women in the developed regions marry between the ages of 20 and 27—on average at age 23—and very early marriages are exceptional. (6) The average age at marriage for women in Latin America and the Caribbean is 22. (7) Except for several Caribbean countries where the age at marriage is unusually high, this average is fairly consistent across the region.

From *The World's Women:* 1970–1990, New York: United Nations, 1991.

Activity 3

Read the information about getting married in the United States. The noun phrases with postmodifiers are underlined. Put a star (★) under the core noun in each of the noun phrases and write *sing.* above the phrase if it is singular and *pl.* if it is plural. The first one is done for you.

sing.
1. Size of the U.S. bridal market: $35 billion
★
2. Average total spending for a formal wedding: $17,470
3. Bride's gown: $850
4. Groom's tuxedo (rental): $110
5. Honeymoon: $3,142
6. Average age in 1955 of a couple marrying for the first time: 21
7. Average age today of a couple marrying for the first time: 26
8. Americans who characterize their marriage as "happy": 97 percent
9. Average length of a marriage ending in a divorce: 7.1 years
10. Chances that a wedding is not the first for either the bride or groom: 1 in 3
11. Estimated number of marriage and family therapists in the United States: 50,000
12. Marriages per week in Las Vegas, Nevada: 1,700

From "Outlook," *U.S. News & World Report,* June 6, 1994.

Activity 4

Individuals/Partners. For this activity, you may want to use a dictionary, such as the *Oxford Advanced Learner's Dictionary* or the *Longman Dictionary of Contemporary English*.

1. Fill in the spaces in the chart. Keep in mind differences between types of nouns. Refer to *The Tapestry Grammar,* Chapter 5, pages 88–93 to review the differences. Try to complete as much as you can on your own before you use a dictionary. Check your work with a partner.

SINGULAR	PLURAL	COUNTABLE/UNCOUNTABLE
age	*ages*	*countable*
analysis		
census		
country		
divorce		
education	*education* or *educations*	*either*
housing		
income		
job		
marriage		
occupation		
residence		
sex		
survey		
work		

2. A few nouns may be either **countable** or **uncountable,** depending on their use (for example, education). For these nouns, write one sentence with its countable meaning and one sentence with its uncountable meaning.

Public universities and private colleges offer different educations. (countable)
Education is a requirement for success. (uncountable)

Lesson 14: Simple Noun Phrases

Definite, Indefinite, and Zero Article—***the other/another/other*** + noun

PREVIEW

Think about your answers to the questions and then discuss them with a partner.

1. What does it mean to be *productive* in life? Try to define or give examples of being productive.
2. During what time of life do you think most people are the most productive? Why?
   a. young adulthood (18–30 years)
   b. early middle age (31–45 years)
   c. late middle age (46–60 years)
   d. older years (61–75 years)
   e. other
3. During what time of life do you expect to be the most productive?
4. In question 2, *the* is used before *most productive* but not before *most people.* What difference in meaning does *the* mark?

PRESENTATION

Simple noun phrases consist of a **determiner + noun.** Although there are many kinds of determiners (articles, "the other/another/other," demonstratives, possessives, and quantifiers), this lesson focuses on the first two: articles and "the other/another/other."

Definite and indefinite articles.

The articles **a/an, the,** and **0** (zero, or no word at all) are the most common fillers of the determiner position. "The" is *definite* because it marks the particular individual(s), thing(s), place(s), or idea(s) named by the noun that follows as "known" to listeners and readers. "A" and "an" are *indefinite* because the noun that follows refers to *any* single thing named by the noun, not one that listeners and readers necessarily "know."

A changes to "an" when the word that follows begins with a vowel sound (**an** appointment, **an** hour, BUT **a** universal [yunɪvɜ́rsəl] question).

1. ***the* + noun** marks a noun as specific (identity is known):
   the student, the books, the classroom, the answer
2. ***a/an* + noun** marks a noun as singular (identity is not known):
   a student, a book, a classroom, an answer

Zero article. **Zero article, *0*,** refers to no article at all. *0* is used with different types of nouns when they refer to the general case. (If you need to review the countable/uncountable distinction, see Lesson 13 or *The Tapestry Grammar*, Chapter 5, p. 91). *0* (zero article) can be used with the following types of nouns:

1. Nouns that are singular, uncountable, and refer to the general case:
   a. Rice is a staple in southern China.
   b. Rice consumption is high in many countries in Asia.
2. Nouns that are plural, countable, and refer to the general case:
   a. Noodles are more common in northern China.
   b. Food preferences vary widely in different parts of China.
3. Nouns that can be either countable or uncountable and refer to the general case:
   a. Climate appears to be a factor in food preferences. (= singular, uncountable, climate in general)
   b. People from hot, humid climates often favor hot, spicy foods. (= plural, countable, hot, humid climates in general)

If you are unsure which article to use, try using the flowchart in Figure 4.1.

FIGURE 4.1

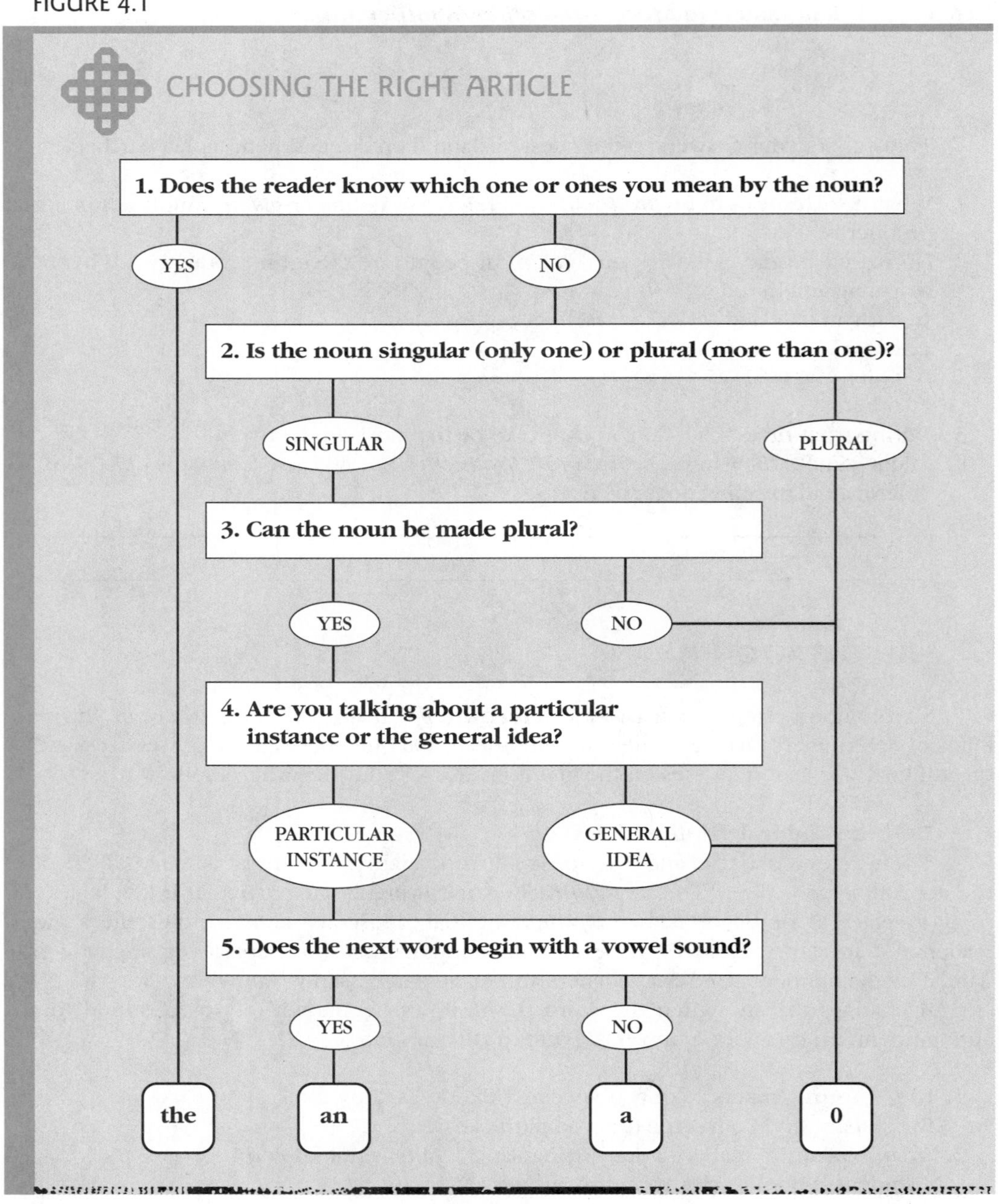

The other/another/other. The difference in meaning between **the other/another/other** is similar to the difference between **the, a/an,** and **0** (zero article).

1. **the other** + noun = the only one(s) left or remaining; a known individual or group (like the definite article "the")
2. **another** + noun = one of many ("an" + "other"); not the only one left (like the indefinite articles "a" and "an")
3. **other** + noun (plural) = several of many, not the only one (like *0,* zero article)

The following passage illustrates these differences:

During the 1980s, the average age of first marriage for women was below 20 years in 24 countries. Fifteen of these countries are in Africa. <u>Another</u> (= one of many (24 countries)) is in the Caribbean. <u>The other</u> (= the remaining ones) eight countries are in Asia. <u>Other</u> (= several of many (countries in general)) Asian countries, such as Japan, have somewhat higher average ages at first marriage.

Adapted from *The World's Women: 1970–1990.* New York: United Nations, 1991.

PRACTICE

Activity 1

Recognizing definite articles. Remember that the definite article "the" indicates that the noun that follows is known to listeners or readers. There are at least seven reasons why the identity of nouns may be known:

1. There is only one in the world (e.g., <u>the</u> sun).
2. There is only one in the physical environment that is understood by listeners and readers (e.g., <u>the</u> hospital in a small town).
3. The noun (or adjective) is used in a general sense to name a social institution (e.g., <u>the</u> family) or a class of individuals (e.g., <u>the</u> computer, to refer to all computers; <u>the</u> poor, to refer to all poor people)
4. The noun has already been mentioned (e.g., first mention: <u>a</u> letter; second and later mention: <u>the</u> letter).
5. The noun has not been mentioned before but is understood from the context (e.g., in a discussion of <u>the</u> hospital, mention of <u>the</u> emergency room).
6. The noun is specified by the noun phrase itself, usually in the postmodifier (e.g., <u>the</u> parents of Nelson Mandela, <u>the</u> child who opened the door).
7. The noun is a proper noun, including nouns that are
   - expanded noun phrases with postmodiers (e.g., <u>the</u> Gulf of Mexico, <u>the</u> United States of America)
   - names of historical events or periods (e.g., <u>the</u> Civil War, <u>the</u> Holocaust, <u>the</u> Cold War era, BUT World War II)
   - plural names of countries and regions (e.g., <u>the</u> Netherlands, <u>the</u> United Kingdom)
   - groups of islands (e.g., <u>the</u> Belearic Islands)
   - ranges of mountains or hills (e.g., <u>the</u> Himalayas)
   - rivers, seas, oceans, canals (e.g., <u>the</u> Nile River)
   - ships (e.g., <u>the</u> Titanic, <u>the</u> Enterprise)
   - newspapers and some organizations (e.g., <u>the</u> London Times, <u>the</u> Sierra Club)
   - some public buildings (e.g., <u>the</u> World Trade Towers, <u>the</u> Taj Majal) but usually not cathedrals, churches, synagogues, or colleges/universities (e.g., St. Peter's Cathedral, Temple Beth El, Michigan State University, BUT <u>the</u> University of Michigan).

Now read the passage on Maggie Kuhn, activist for the elderly. There are numbered blanks before all the definite articles (*the*) in the passage. Write the number of the reason for the use of *the* in the blank. (This will help you understand when to use *the*.) In some cases there may be more than one reason. You may want to complete the first two paragraphs with your class or a partner before you complete the rest of the passage on your own.

MAGGIE KUHN, ACTIVIST FOR ______ (1) THE ELDERLY

PHILADELPHIA—Maggie Kuhn, 89, who decided retirement age was no reason to give up and helped found ______ (2) the **Gray Panthers** as a tool against discrimination and ______ (3) the Vietnam War, has died. Kuhn died Saturday at home in her nurse's arms, said her personal secretary, Sue Leary.

"She had always said she wanted to die before she reached ______ (4) the age of 90 and she was going to turn 90 in August. She kind of died her way," said Laura Quinn, who helped Kuhn write her autobiography, *No Stone Unturned:* ______ (5) *The Life and Times of Maggie Kuhn.*

______ (6) The country is losing one of its most **indefatigable** activists," Quinn said. "She **epitomized** ______ (7) the power of ______ (8) the **grass roots.** She's just a charming person who with **pithy** sayings and incredible determination changed ______ (9) the way everyone thought about old age." Kuhn was one of five women who founded ______ (10) the Gray Panthers 25 years ago. She said she got involved after being forced to retire from ______ (11) the United Presbyterian Office of Church and Society at age 65.

In a 1989 interview, she said ______ (12) the world unfairly portrays ______ (13) the old as weak. ______ (14) "The first myth is that old age is a disease, a terrible disease that you never admit you've got, so you lie about your age," she said. "Well, it's not a disease—it's a **triumph.** Because you've survived. Failure, disappointment, sickness, loss—you're still here."

But ______ (15) the group's first organizing issue was U.S. involvement in ______ (16) the Vietnam War. "That issue identified us with ______ (17) the young," she said. ______ (18) The Panthers also turned to several other social issues, battling sexism and racial injustice.

Abridged from A. Westfeldt, "Maggie Kuhn, Activist for Elderly, Gray Panther Founder, Dies at 89." *Wisconsin State Journal,* April 23, 1995.

activist someone involved in social change
Gray Panthers an organization of older or retired individuals; modeled after the Black Panthers, a militant organization of African Americans most active during the 1960s
indefatigable incapable of being tired; tireless
epitomize be a typical example of
grass roots people at the local level rather than people at the center of power
pithy to the point, short and meaningful
triumph a big victory; an event worthy of public celebration

Activity 2

Partners. Reread the last two paragraphs of the passage from Activity 1. Write a zero (0) above every noun phrase that has a zero article and does not have any other kind of determiner. (You should have eight zeros.) With a partner, discuss why the zero article was used in these noun phrases.

Activity 3

Recognizing articles (Partners). Read the final paragraphs below of "Maggie Kuhn, Activist for the Elderly." Circle every article (*the, a/an*) you find. With a partner, try to explain why the definite or indefinite article was used.

(1) The [Gray] Panthers now have more than 40,000 members in 32 states and six countries. (2) Only one of the founders, Polly Cuthbertson, is alive, in a Philadelphia retirement home.

(3) Kuhn's autobiography told her story against the backdrop of 20th-century changes: the women's movement, the peace movement, the civil rights movement, and the environmental movement. (4) It included a frank discussion of her sexual and romantic encounters. (5) Kuhn, who never married, wrote of a 15-year relationship with a married minister and an affair with a man 50 years her junior she met when he was a University of Washington student. (6) She had written that she would like her gravestone inscribed: "Here lies Maggie Kuhn under the only stone she left unturned."

Activity 4

Choosing the right article. In the passage "Law and Order," there are blanks in place of all the articles (*the, a/an*) that the author originally used. A blank is also placed where the author used a zero article. Read the passage and fill in the blanks with an appropriate article, using *0* for zero article. You may want to use Figure 4.1 to help you decide which article to use. In some cases, more than one article is possible.

HINT In the original version, five zero articles were used.

LAW AND ORDER: BILINGUAL OFFICER SERVING AS ROLE MODEL

When Beloit Police Officer Antonio Matos was ______ (1) young boy, he watched his father, ______ (2) cab driver in New York, get up at 5 A.M. six or seven days ______ (3) week to go to ______ (4) work. Often, his dad did not come home again until midnight.

"I saw how hard he had to work, and I knew I needed to get ______ (5) education to get ahead," said Matos, who was born in ______ (6) Dominican Republic and grew up in ______ (7) Bronx. "My family always stressed ______ (8) education. Even though he didn't go to ______ (9) college, my father always told me how important it was for me to get ______ (10) education."

Matos, 27, is ______ (11) first person in his family to graduate from college. He first earned ______ (12) associate degree in ______ (13) aerospace technology. He then earned ______ (14) bachelor's degree in ______ (15) industrial engineering. His next goal is ______ (16) law degree.

Matos joined ______ (17) Beloit Police Department last May. He is ______ (18) first and only Beloit police officer who speaks Spanish fluently.

Antonio Matos

Abridged from M. K. Cunningham, "Law and Order: Bilingual Officer Serving as Role Model for City Youth." *Beloit Daily News,* March 2. 1995. Photo by Chris Kelley.

Activity 5

Choosing the right article. Read some additional paragraphs from the passage, "Law and Order." As in Activity 4, fill in an appropriate article (*the, a/an,* or *0*) in the blanks. In some cases, more than one article is possible.

(1) ______ (1) road to success for Matos has not been easy. ______ (2) violence was ______ (3) part of ______ (4) daily life in ______ (5) Bronx. "It was rough in my neighborhood. There were ______ (6) **shootouts** almost every night," he said.

However, there were ______ (7) good things in his life to keep him out of ______ (8) trouble. "Even though there were all those negative influences, there were so many positive influences. You had all kinds of art museums and culture. There was ______ (9) Central Park. There were ______ (10) Boys Clubs every 10 blocks in New York. If you were getting into ______ (11) trouble, it wasn't because you didn't have ______ (12) choice. It was because you almost want[ed] to get into ______ (13) trouble. Because you [didn't] care," he said.

His family also was ______ (14) influence in his life. His parents were not married, and when he was young, he lived with his grandmother and uncles. "I didn't come from your traditional nuclear family. I didn't see that as bad. I thought of it as my whole family coming together to take care of me. My father was always there for me financially," he added.

As ______ (15) Beloit police officer, Matos translates for other police officers while he is on duty. When he is off duty, he carries ______ (16) **beeper** in case his bilingual skills are needed.

Matos said he tries to take ______ (17) **laid-back** approach to his job. For instance, he said he tries to talk to ______ (18) young people and help them understand ______ (19) options they have. "I believe that ______ (20) law enforcement officer, or ______ (21) teacher or anyone in ______ (22) community should take ______ (23) time to be ______ (24) role model to ______ (25) young people."

Matos **takes to heart** ______ (26) African proverb, "It takes ______ (27) entire village to raise ______ (28) child." He is trying to get involved with ______ (29) mentoring groups so he can help ______ (30) young people. He and other African-American officers have begun talking to ______ (31) different groups in ______ (32) community.

shootouts gun fights between opposing groups
beeper a small electronic device that sends a signal when the person carrying it is contacted
laid-back relaxed, flexible
take to heart take seriously

Activity 6

The other/another/other. Read the following two sentences, which are the same except for the addition of *the* in (1a):

1. **a.** Matos and the other African-American officers have begun talking to different groups in the community.
   b. Matos and other African-American officers have begun talking to different groups in the community.
   What is the difference in meaning between the two sentences?
   ____
   ____

2. Reread the passages on "Law and Order" in Activities 4 and 5. Think about Antonio Matos's growing up in a bad neighborhood in the Bronx, New York. In spite of a difficult childhood, Matos graduated from college and began a successful career as a bilingual police officer. Why do you think Matos succeeded when other young people from similar backgrounds fail? Write five reasons for his success. Use "another," and "the other" appropriately.
   a. One reason is that ______________________________
   b. Another reason ______________________________
   c. ______________________________
   d. ______________________________
   e. ______________________________

Activity 7

The other/another/other (Partners/Whole class).

1. Choose one of the following topics and think of three or four reasons why you are (not) doing it or (not) going to do it. Use another, the other whenever you can.

   Study English — Work part-time — Travel across the country
   Get a job — Get a pet — Get married — Your choice of topic

   a. ______________________________
   b. ______________________________
   c. ______________________________
   d. ______________________________

2. Interview your partner about his or her topic and write down the reasons he or she gave for doing it now or in the future. Use another, the other whenever you can.
   Topic: ______________________________
   a. ______________________________
   b. ______________________________
   c. ______________________________
   d. ______________________________

3. As a class, choose one of the topics in (1) and brainstorm to come up with as many reasons as possible for and against it. Then group similar reasons together and write sentences that describe each of the groups. For example:
   a. *These reasons all have to do with (describe).*
   b. *Some other reasons*
   c. *The other reasons*

Lesson 15: Simple Noun Phrases

Definite/Indefinite Quantifiers + Noun

PREVIEW

Read the following passage and then answer the questions.

(1) Carol O'Neill never worried that her sexual orientation might cost her her job. (2) A single mother, she was much more concerned about whether she was making enough in tips to pay the rent and keep her three **rambunctious** little boys in tennis shoes. (3) O'Neill earned good money **tending bar** in a nightclub called the Late Show in New Port Richey, a town on Florida's Gulf Coast just north of Tampa Bay. (4) The club was struggling, though, and the owner decided to try to **draw** a different crowd. (5) In mid-December, owner Audrey McGillivray informed O'Neill that in <u>three</u> days she'd be **out of a job,** O'Neill recalls. (6) Also let go were the club's cocktail waitresses, Judy Whyte and Julie Meindersma, and its other bartender, Kathleen Shappell.

(7) <u>All</u> <u>four</u> fired workers are **straight**. (8) The club was being turned into a **gay** bar. (9) O'Neill and her former co-workers say they're quite comfortable around gay people. (10) What made them awfully uncomfortable was losing their jobs.

Excerpted from Deb Price, "U.S. Job Law Needed by Gays and Straights," *Minneapolis Star Tribune,* May 25, 1994.

rambunctious active, very energetic
tending bar to work as a bartender (to prepare drinks in a bar)
draw attract
be out of a job to be fired from a job; to let someone go
straight heterosexual orientation
gay homosexual, often referring to males; lesbian, when referring to females

FOR YOUR INFORMATION According to the article cited above, Federal job protection categories now include race, color, religion, national origin, gender, age, and disability. Although <u>more than 80</u> cities and counties in the United States also cover sexual orientation, only <u>eight</u> states do.

1. Is what happened to O'Neill and her co-workers fair? Is it legal?
2. What would you do if you were O'Neill?
3. If O'Neill were fired from the same job because she was a lesbian, would that be fair?

In the passage in the Preview, all the underlined words are **quantifiers,** words that describe how much there is or how many there are of the core noun. Different quantifiers may be used with countable and uncountable nouns and in formal and informal writing/speech.

PRESENTATION

Quantifiers can be divided into four groups: definite, indefinite, negative, and comparative. This lesson covers the first two groups, definite and indefinite. **Definite** quantifiers

- give an exact number or idea of the core noun that follows, for example, <u>four</u> weeks, <u>1,000</u> catalogs, <u>every</u> purchase
- include all numbers and words that specify number, for example, <u>four</u>, <u>fifty</u>, <u>both</u>, <u>either</u>, <u>all</u>, <u>each</u>, <u>every</u>
- may occur as predeterminers before determiners, for example, <u>all</u> the problems, <u>both</u> the buyers and the salespeople

In contrast, **indefinite** quantifiers

- give an inexact idea of quantities, for example, some items, a lot of information, many refunds, a great deal of time
- may vary in formality, for example, a lot of time (informal), a great deal of time (formal)

Some definite and indefinite quantifiers

- may move into the premodifier position if they are preceded by a determiner:
  the first 100 customers, their many complaints
  [determiner] [premodifier] [determiner] [premodifier]
- may occur with *of*-phrases, for example, all of the time, most of the time, some of the time
- are restricted in their use with countable/uncountable nouns and in formal writing

TABLE 4.4 sums up restrictions on the use of definite and indefinite quantifiers with countable/uncountable nouns and in formal writing.

TABLE 4.4 Quantifiers

	WITH SINGULAR COUNTABLE NOUNS	WITH PLURAL NOUNS	WITH UNCOUNTABLE NOUNS	IN FORMAL WRITING
Definite quantifiers				
one	yes	no	no	yes
two, three, etc.	no	yes	no	yes
both (the, etc.)	no	yes	no	yes
either (the, etc.)	yes	yes	yes	yes
all (the, etc.)	no	yes	yes	yes
each	yes	no	no	yes
every	yes	no	no	yes
Indefinite quantifiers				
any	yes	yes	yes	yes
some	no	yes	yes	yes
a lot of/lots of	no	yes	yes	no
a couple of (the, etc.)	no	yes	no	no
a few	no	yes	no	yes
several	no	yes	no	yes
many	no	yes	no	yes
a little	no*	no	yes	yes

**Little* is also used as an adjective meaning "small." In that sense, it can be used with both singular and plural countable nouns, e.g., "a little job," "some little jobs."

PRACTICE

Activity 1

Read the following paragraphs from the article "U.S. Job Law Needed by Gays and Straights." Definite and indefinite quantifiers and other determiners are underlined in the passage. List the underlined words under the appropriate category at the end of the article.

In reviewing 20 surveys conducted since 1980, the National Gay and Lesbian Task Force found that between 16 percent and 44 percent of gay people have **confronted** employment discrimination. Some bosses are quite open about not wanting gay workers: among employers in Anchorage, Alaska, who do not have a gay friend or relative, 57 percent told **pollsters** in 1988 that they would not hire anyone gay and 40 percent said they'd fire gay employees.

Most Americans find such prejudice **distasteful**. In **poll** after poll, three-fourths oppose job **bias** against gay people. Yet any requests for passage of civil rights laws to protect workers against discrimination based on sexual orientation are often misheard as demands for "special"—not equal—rights. That misunderstanding arises because only 30 percent of Americans realize that gay workers aren't already protected by federal law (Mellman, Lazarus, Lake, Inc., poll, February 1994). Neither are straight workers.

Slightly adapted from Deb Price, "U.S. Job Law Needed by Gays and Straights," *Minneapolis Star Tribune,* May 25, 1994.

confront face, encounter
pollster a person who surveys public opinion
distasteful unpleasant or disagreeable
poll a survey of people's responses to questions
bias a preference in favor or against something

Definite quantifiers	**Indefinite quantifiers**	**Other determiners**
____________	____________	____________
____________	____________	____________
____________	____________	____________

Activity 2

Partners. The following quantifiers are listed in alphabetical order. List them in order of increasing size of quantity. Discuss any disagreements with a partner and then compare your answers with others in the class.

a few, the majority of, most[1], several, all, many, no[2], some

1 ____________________ smallest quantity
2. ____________________
3. ____________________
4. ____________________
5. ____________________
6. ____________________
7. ____________________
8. ____________________ largest quantity

[1]A comparative quantifier.
[2]A negative quantifier.

Activity 3

Group. As a group, take a survey of your class's or another group's attitudes about hiring or firing people based on sexual orientation. (To encourage more honest answers, you may want to do this in writing and ask about general attitudes in a particular country instead of asking for personal opinions.) Here are some possible questions to include in your survey. If you prefer, write your own questions.

How would people in your home country generally respond to these questions?

1. Should employers be able to hire workers based on sexual orientation (instead of their qualifications)?

   ________ Yes ________ No ________ Don't know
2. Should employers be able to fire workers based on sexual orientation (instead of their job performance)?

   ________ Yes ________ No ________ Don't know

3. Are there any jobs or careers that should *only* be open to individuals with a certain sexual orientation?

_______ Yes _______ No _______ Don't know

If yes, what jobs or careers? ______________________________

____

4. Should there be a federal law that protects workers against discrimination based on sexual preference? (U.S. federal law only protects workers against discrimination based on race, color, religion, national origin, sex, age, and disability.)

_______ Yes _______ No _______ Don't know

OPTIONAL After surveying at least 10 people, summarize your responses by calculating the percentage for each answer in each question. Then describe each percentage by using an appropriate quantifier, such as, no, a few, several, some, many, the majority of, most, or all. For example:

Question	Percentage of responses (out of 10 responses)	Possible quantifier
1.	Yes: 20%	a couple of
	No: 30%	some
	Don't know: 50%	many

Activity 4

A few quantifiers are similar in meaning but differ in degree of formality. Table 4.5 summarizes these differences and lists other quantifiers and adjectives that are similar in meaning.

TABLE 4.5 Comparison of Formal and Informal Uses of Quantifiers

QUANTIFIER INFORMAL USE (Speech or writing)	QUANTIFIER MORE FORMAL USE (Speech or writing)	ADJECTIVE MORE FORMAL USE (Speech or writing)
a couple of + countable noun (may be used to refer to two or three things)	two a pair of (two items in a set, e.g. a pair of socks)	dual (in special cases, e.g., dual brakes, a dual income family)
a lot of/lots of + uncountable noun (not) much of + uncountable noun a lot of/lots of + countable noun	(not) a great deal of (not) a large amount of many a large number of	considerable substantial

The following sentences come from an informal class discussion about a survey. Change the underlined quantifiers to more formal words or phrases to communicate the same information in academic writing.

1. People didn't understand the first couple of questions.
2. Lots of people didn't know how to answer question 3.
3. There was a lot of confusion about the meaning of some of the words.
4. There was a lot of disagreement about when employers should fire people.
5. A couple of people thought that firing a single parent (mother or father) and firing an adult (non-parent) wasn't the same.
6. The survey resulted in a lot of discussion by the class.

Activity 5

Individuals/Partners. What do the notes on a refrigerator door say about someone? They can reveal a lot about what people like to do and what they value, according to Mary Dikkeboom, a home economist with the UW-Extension in Rock County, Wisconsin.

1. Read the list of items on Betsy Ahner's refrigerator and fill in an appropriate article or quantifier in the blank before each item. Remember that zero article (0) counts as an article. In some cases, more than one answer is possible. Then try to answer the question at the end. Compare answers with a partner.

   a. On the left side of the refrigerator

   ____________ Austin's Barber Shop calendar

   ____________ Ewald Vision magnet

   ____________ high school's final exam schedule

   ____________ assorted school papers

   b. On the front side

   ____________ recyling information

   ____________ Laidlaw (recyling pick-up company) magnet

   ____________ assorted phone numbers of her children's friends

   ____________ sports physical card that needs to be completed

   ____________ list of her daughter's favorite rock bands and groups

   ____________ fingerprints in jam and catsup colors

   c. On the right side

   ____________ suction cups with hooks to hold dish towels

From "Refrigerator Psychology," *Beloit Daily News,* Feb. 4, 1994.

What do the contents on Betsy Ahner's refrigerator say about her?

____

____

____

2. Make a list of what you have on your refrigerator's door (or a friend's), using appropriate articles or quantifiers. Interview a partner about his or her refrigerator and take notes. Begin by asking questions about the following: lists, magnets, notices, pictures, cartoons, schedules, children's artwork, special items:

   EXAMPLE Do you have any lists on your refrigerator?

Write a short paragraph about your partner's refrigerator's door and then write a sentence or two about what these items tell you about your partner.

Lesson 16: Wh-clauses

Relative Clauses as Postmodifiers

PREVIEW

Think about your answers to the following questions and then discuss them with a partner.

1. What is one experience that has significantly changed your life?
2. Have you ever heard an important prediction that later came true? If so, what was the prediction?
3. Certain animals are important symbols in different cultures (e.g., the spider among the Ashanti of central Ghana). What is one animal that is a well-known symbol in your native culture?

PRESENTATION

Each of the preceding questions contains a ***wh*-clause,** or a **relative clause.** A *wh*-clause adds identifying information about or defines more precisely the core noun that it follows. ***Wh*-clauses** are generally introduced with *that* or one of the following ***wh*-words** (relative pronouns): *who, whom, which, when, where, whose*. Underline the *wh*-clauses in the Preview questions.

Quick Review. Although there are several types of wh-clauses, this lesson focuses on just two: (1) wh-clauses in which the core noun is the subject of the clause and (2) wh-clauses in which the core noun is the object of the clause. Here is an example of each.

1. The core noun is the subject of the *wh*-clause:
   One experience that has significantly changed my life is living abroad.
   - Identifying statement — **One experience** has significantly changed my life.
     subject (becomes relative clause):
     One experience ⟶ that
   - Main statement: — One experience is living abroad.
   - Identifying + main statement: — One experience **that has significantly changed my life** is living abroad.
2. The core noun is the object of the *wh*-clause:
   An important lesson that I learned was to be flexible.
   - Identifying statement: — I learned **an important lesson.**
     object (becomes relative clause):
     an important lesson ⟶ **that**
   - Main statement: — An important lesson was to be flexible.
   - Identifying + main statement: — An important lesson **(that) I learned** was to be flexible.

NOTE In informal speech and writing, the *wh*-words *that* and *who* are usually left out when the core noun is the object (in the predicate) of the identifying statement. See the sentence in (2).

For additional information about relative clauses, see *The Tapestry Grammar,* Chapter 6, pages 134–143.

LEARNING STRATEGY

Forming Concepts: Analyzing new information and reviewing old information helps you understand it better.

PRACTICE

Activity 1

Table 4.6 lists common *wh*-words and their uses in *wh*-clauses (relative clauses). Review the table and then complete the activity below.

TABLE 4.6 Common *Wh*-Words and Their Uses

WH-WORD	USE
who	introduces clauses that identify people only
which	introduces clauses that identify things only
that	introduces clauses that identify people or things; with people, *that* is more informal
0 (zero)	introduces clauses that identify people or things, but ONLY when they are in the object (predicate) of the identifying statement
where	introduces clauses that identify places; replaces *there* or prepositional phrases meaning *in/on/at* a place
when	introduces clauses that identify a time; replaces *then* or prepositional phrases meaning *in/on/at* a time

Read about an event that changed the lives of David and Valerie Heider in 1994. Underline the *wh*-clauses in the passage and circle the *wh*-words that introduce them. Write a 0 above any *wh*-clauses where there is no *wh*-word.

A MODERN-DAY "MIRACLE"

(1) Making a bed of **brush** beneath a row of trees, the soon-to-be mother prepared to give birth. (2) Under the blanket of a Wisconsin night, she began to **labor** in the quiet pasture. (3) Assisted by only the spirits of nature, a new life was about to begin. (4) The next morning, she **cradled** the newborn close to her body, protective and proud of the life she had created, not realizing the miracle she had accomplished.

(5) In the weeks that followed, thousands of people from across the world would travel to the 45-acre **exotic game farm** in Janesville, Wisconsin, visiting the pasture where the **heralded** birth occurred. (6) Like pilgrims on a religious journey, many would bring gifts; others came to pray. (7) All wanted to share in what many call "a modern-day miracle."

(8) It was the morning of August 20, 1994, when David Heider first **laid eyes on** something so rare that animal experts had believed it was impossible. (9) Along the edge of the fence line, Heider watched as the newborn buffalo calf **suckled** her mother. (10) In disbelief, he stared at the calf's white coat. (11) So rare was her birth, bison experts had estimated the odds at 1 in 10 million. (12) Many in the industry had believed the gene that produces the white coat had been lost when the buffalo nearly became extinct in the 1890s.

Miracle: The White Buffalo at Eight Days.

Source: White Buffalo Inc., Janesville, WI. Reprinted by permission.

(13) David, along with his wife Valerie and son Corey, soon began to realize the importance of the calf's birth and its impact on others. (14) They discovered the **phenomenal** birth has spiritual meaning to Native Americans. (15) To those who believe in their culture, the birth of the white calf is a **prophecy** come true and a time of great spiritual healing. (16) Honoring those beliefs, the Heiders opened their farm to all who wanted to share in something so rare. (17) Within the first two months after its birth, more than 10,000 people had visited the farm. (18) Many, upon seeing the calf for the first time, said they were overcome with emotion. (19) Even members of the media have reported a sense of peace and tranquility they **attribute** to seeing the calf. (20) Watching the calf touch so many lives, the Heiders decided "Miracle" was the only suitable name for her.

Slightly adapted from Neal White, "A Modern Day 'Miracle,'" unpublished description of the authorized painting of Miracle, by Gary Gandy, n.d.

brush thick growth of bushes or shrubs
labor give birth
cradle to hold close
exotic game farm farm with wild animals from unfamiliar places that are usually hunted for food or sport in their native lands
heralded (adj.) announced as important
lay eyes on see
suckle to take in milk; nurse
phenomenal incredible
prophecy a prediction, often of a religious nature
attribute give credit to; associate with

Activity 2

Give identifying information or definitions for the following word(s) from the passage in Activity 1. Use *wh*-clauses in your sentences. Two are done for you as examples.

1. August 20, 1994
2. miracle
3. pasture
4. calf
5. extinct
6. David Heider
7. exotic game farm
8. tranquility
9. Native Americans
10. suitable

1. *August 20, 1994, is the date when Miracle was born.*
2. ______
3. ______
4. ______
5. *Extinct is an adjective that means no longer living.*
6. ______
7. ______
8. ______
9. ______
10. ______

Activity 3

The use of the word *that* can be confusing because it has several meanings and uses in English. For example, *that* can be

1. a demonstrative (*that* time, *that* place)
2. a *wh*-word in relative clauses (the event *that* changed the Heiders' lives)
3. a subordinator in a subordinate clause after a verb (The Heiders understood *that* Miracle was a spiritual sign in Sioux culture.)

Read the following passage, in which all examples of *that* are underlined. Refer to the above list and write 1, 2, or 3 above each underlined *that* to identify its use.

LOOKING HORSE FAMILY—KEEPERS OF ORIGINAL LAKOTA SACRED PIPE

For 18 generations Arbol's family had served as the protector of both the future and the past. It was his grandmother's final dream in life to see (1) that responsibility become his. He was only 12 years old when (2) that trust was passed down at her deathbed.

Twenty-eight years later in rural Janesville, Dr. Arbol Looking Horse, Keeper of the Sacred Pipe, nineteenth generation, watched his family's destiny unfold. Centuries ago, legends say (3) that the spirit of the White Buffalo Calf Woman came to the Lakota Sioux and presented them with a sacred pipe, which was to be used to bring peace to the fighting nations. The elders of the different nations gathered and smoked from the pipe. After a period of harmony, it was told (4) that dissension would return. After many years of disagreement and destruction, the spirit of the White Buffalo Calf Woman would return, and the nations would be joined once again. Since (5) that time, members of the Looking Horse family, based in Pine Fork, South Dakota, have protected the sacred pipe.

The prophecies (6) that are being fulfilled are starting to show "a coming together of people going back to their natural ways," said Looking Horse, as he prepared for the unification ceremony. Looking Horse explained (7) that in these times, the white buffalo calf "is like an oasis of divine intervention coming up from Mother Earth."

"The things (8) that the elders have talked about for so long, now we can identify with what we have been taught," he said. "We are given this to strengthen each other. This is an important time in history."

Slightly adapted from Neal White,
"Looking Horse Family—Keepers of Original Lakota Sacred Pipe,"
Beloit Daily News, Sept. 13, 1994.

Activity 4

Individuals/Partners. Combine the pairs of statements that follow so that the first (identifying) statement is combined into the second (main) statement as a *wh*-clause. The first one is done for you. Compare your sentences with a partner's sentences. In which sentences could you omit a *wh*-word in the relative clause?

1. Winona LaDuke wears shocking purple and turquoise cowboy boots.
   Winona LaDuke, 35, is a nationally known Native American activist.

   Winona LaDuke, 35, is a nationally known Native American activist who wears shocking purple and turquoise cowboy boots.

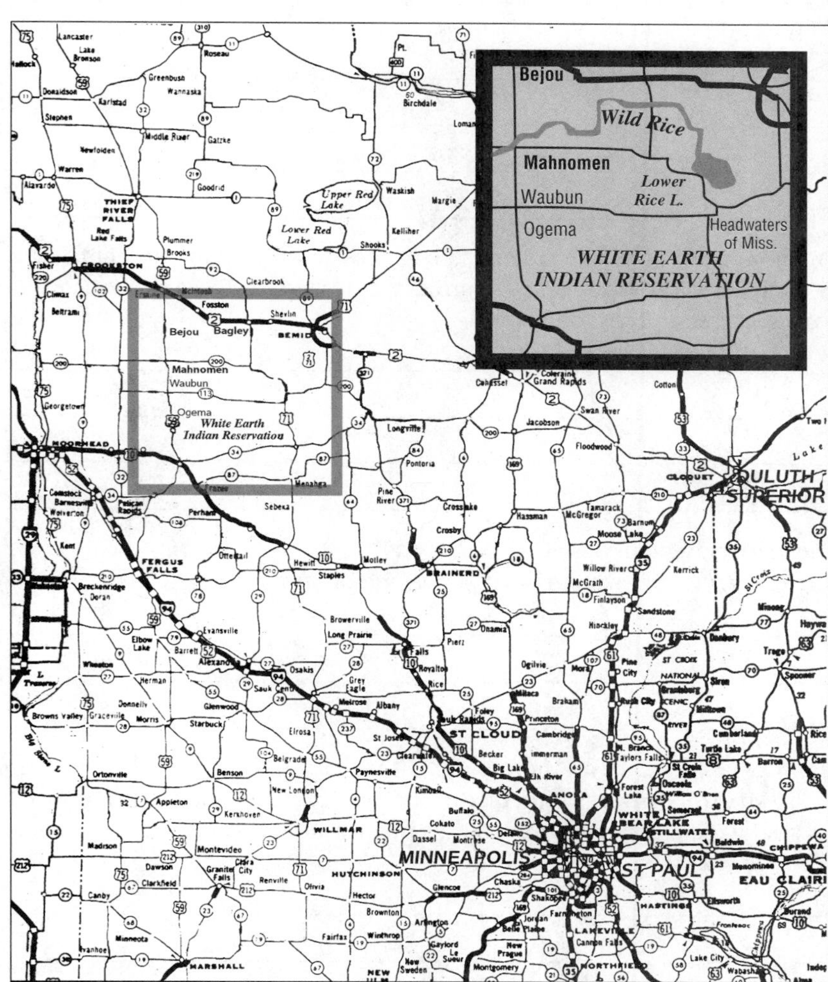

Map of Minnesota detailing White Earth Indian Reservation (north of Detroit Lakes).

2. She caught the frozen whitefish on Round Lake on Northern Minnesota's White Earth Indian Reservation.
   In her kitchen, she is up to her elbows in the frozen whitefish.

3. The Ojibway once owned all the land in the reservation.
As director of the White Earth Land Recovery Project, LaDuke wants to buy back—or reclaim—all the land.

4. LaDuke lives there.
The White Earth Band of Ojibway today holds about 60,000 acres of the 837,000-acre reservation.

5. The legislation would return more than 45,000 acres of federally owned land in the reservation to the Ojibway.
In 1993 the White Earth Land Recovery Project asked U.S. Senator Paul Wellstone (Minnesota) to introduce legislation.

6. The nonprofit foundation focuses on American Indian environmental issues.
In addition to the land-recovery project, LaDuke is a Greenpeace board member and works for a nonprofit foundation.

7. The leaders were under 40.
In 1994, *Time* magazine named her as one of 50 emerging leaders.

8. Ojibway children attend there.
As a Harvard University graduate, LaDuke receives many invitations to speak at prestigious colleges and universities but would rather speak at the tribal school on White Earth.

Slightly adapted from Susan M. Barbieri, "Thunderbird Woman Lands," *St. Paul Pioneer Press,* May 28, 1995.

LEARNING STRATEGY

Managing Your Learning: Talking to a partner about your ideas is a good way to test your understanding.

Activity 5

Read the passage from "Thunderbird Woman Lands." Fill in the blanks with one or more appropriate *wh*-words. Include 0 (zero *wh*-word) if possible. Be ready to give reasons for your answers.

Winona LaDuke's Ojibway name is "Benaysayequay," __________ (1) is Ojibway for "thunderbird woman." According to American Indian beliefs, the thunderbird is an enormous creature __________ (2) brings thunder, lightning, and rain. Her late father was Ojibway, and her mother is a Russian Jew. She was raised near a reservation in Ashland, Oregon, a town __________ (3) had no Jews and few Indians.

"I was the darkest kid in the class—the one __________ (4) was never asked to dance, the one __________ (5) was never picked for teams, the one __________ (6) was punished by teachers, the one __________ (7) didn't get asked to the high-school prom. So I don't have an [early] experience of being accepted," she says.

For a short time the family lived in the barrio of East Los Angeles, __________ (8) LaDuke's father, an actor and new-age author named Sun Bear, worked as an extra in Western movies. LaDuke's parents also worked to help migrant farm workers, and LaDuke often was taken out of school to attend civil rights and anti-war demonstrations.

After graduating from high school, LaDuke spent five years working for a variety of American Indian organizations on reservations in the western and plains states. She met a Cree man with whom she had two children, __________ (9) are now ages 6 and 4. Inspired by her mother, an art professor in Oregon __________ (10) paints and writes books about Third World women and art, LaDuke obtained scholarships and worked her way through college at Harvard University. Not surprisingly, the field __________ (11) she chose was native economic development. After graduating in 1992, she moved to White Earth. For the first time in her life, she felt welcome. White Earth was home.

Slightly adapted from Susan M. Barbieri, "Thunderbird Woman Lands," *St. Paul Pioneer Press,* May 28, 1995.

Lesson 17: Choosing the Right Article

the, a/an, or zero (***0***) article

PREVIEW

1. In your class or with another group of people, find a person who
   - always arrives on time
   - likes to play team sports
   - would rather watch sports than play them
   - always eats breakfast
   - is a vegetarian
   - has climbed a mountain
   - likes jazz music
2. Did you find more than one person in any of the above categories?
3. Can you explain the difference in meaning between the sentences in (a) and (b)?
   a. Find a person who always arrives on time.
   b. Find the person who always arrives on time.

   ____

   ____

PRESENTATION

In both sentences (a) and (b), the *wh*-clause (relative clause) gives additional information about the core noun *person*. But in (a) the indefinite article "a" before the noun identifies it as one of many possible persons (or at least more than one). As a result, the *wh*-clause that follows simply gives added information about the core noun. In (b), the definite article "the" before *person* identifies it as known, and the *wh*-clause that follows further defines *person* as a unique individual in that context, the *only* person who always arrives on time. In other words, in this context

- <u>a</u> person who always arrives on time → identity unknown; could identify one or more people
- <u>the</u> person who always arrives on time → understood to be one person

PRACTICE

Activity 1

Partners. Read the following situations and write in the appropriate article, *a/an* or *the,* in the blanks. In some cases, more than one article is possible. Compare your answers with a partner's. Discuss any differences in your answers.

1. You've just arrived at the scene of an accident. Several people are standing around _______ young man who has fallen off his bicycle head first. His chin is bleeding badly. You ask, "Has anybody called _______ ambulance?"
2. You're _______ big fan of tennis and never miss _______ important match when _______ Wimbledon games are on TV. You were especially looking forward to seeing _______ men's semi-final match. Unfortunately, you locked yourself out of your apartment and missed _______ match.

3. You're new in _______ town of 35,000 and are attending _______ social gathering at work. It's allergy season and you're suffering from hayfever and other problems. You turn to _______ colleague who has been friendly to you and ask, "Is there _______ allergist in town?"
4. Your colleague in (3) doesn't have allergies, but his wife does. You find out there are two allergists in town because your colleague's wife asks you, "Do you want _______ allergist at City Clinic or _______ one at Riverview Clinic?" Then she adds, "if you need _______ allergist for children, I'd recommend _______ one at City Clinic.
5. You're _______ vegetarian and you're waiting for your meal on an airplane. You're _______ only one not eating Salisbury steak or grilled peppercorn chicken. You overhear _______ flight attendant with _______ meal in her hand say to another, "Where's _______ vegetarian?"
6. You've arrived at your destination, have spent _______ restless night in _______ hotel your friend recommended, and are ready for breakfast. You read _______ menu, which has four choices. Your server suddenly appears and asks if you want _______ continental, _______ buffet breakfast, _______ businessman's special, or two eggs any style. You smile weakly and ask for some coffee.

Activity 2

Read about the journey of Alvin Straight, who uses a tractor lawn mower to get around. Write in the appropriate article, *a/an* or *the*, in the blanks. In cases where more than one article is possible, both are included. Be prepared to explain any difference in meaning in these cases.

BLUE RIVER, WI (AP)—_______ (1) 73-year-old Iowa man wanted to visit _______ (2) brother in Wisconsin but lacked _______ (3) driver's license, so he overcame that obstacle by making _______ (4) 240-mile trip aboard _______ (5) tractor lawn mower. Alvin Straight of Laurens was only part way along on his **itinerary** to reach his brother's home near Blue River when _______ (6) mower broke down. Up until then it was _______ (7) fine trip, he said.

"Taking (a/the) _______ (8) bus, you go too **darned** fast. You can't see _______ (9) country going though," Straight said. "And as far as flying, I did enough of that in World War II."

Alvin learned this summer that Henry Straight, 80, suffered _______ (10) stroke. He wanted to make _______ (11) trip on his Ariens mower. It broke down, so he bought _______ (12) second-hand 1966 John Deere mower, got _______ (13) 10-foot trailer to haul gasoline, clothes, food, and camping equipment, then left July 5 just after his Social Security check arrived.

"I thought I was taking (a/the) ______ (14) short way to my brother's," he said. "I took ______ (15) long way. ______ (16) long way and (0/the) ______ (17) rough way."

On (0/the) ______ (18) good days, he averaged about five miles an hour along U.S. (Highway) 18. He thinks ______ (19) mower holds five quarts of gasoline and made about 32 miles per tankful. He had to be off ______ (20) road by sundown because ______ (21) mower doesn't have headlights. About four days into his trip, ______ (22) Deere's engine failed in West Bend, just 21 miles out of Laurens. He spent $250 replacing ______ (23) points, condenser, plugs, generator, and starter. His limited budget was nearly exhausted. That meant camping wherever he stopped along ______ (24) highway. Was he worried about safety?

"What would I be scared of? Hell, I went through combat in World War II. They ain't going to show me ______ (25) darned thing I ain't seen before," he said. "I've got two good **canes.**"

Excerpted from "Iowa Man Drives Mower 240 Miles," *Beloit Daily News,* Aug. 24, 1994.

itinerary the route of a trip or journey
darn an acceptable alternative to *damn,* an offensive term
cane a stick used as an aid in walking

Activity 3

You've just won a Fabulous Fun Weekend for two in the Lifestyles of the Not-So-Rich-and-Famous Sweepstakes. Choose *five* of the following attractions to visit in Milwaukee (Wisconsin). Read the descriptions and rate your choices from 1 to 5 (1 = top choice) in the blanks before each number. Write in an appropriate article (*a/an, the,* or *0*) in the blanks of the descriptions. You may want to review articles with place names from Lesson 14 or *The Tapestry Grammar,* Chapter 5, Figure 5-7, pages 99–100, before you begin.

FOR YOUR INFORMATION *Lifestyles of the Rich and Famous* is a TV program that features the lives of wealthy people in their expensive homes or favorite vacation spots all over the world.

____ **1.** *Milwaukee County Zoo.* ________ black rhino, hyenas, jaguars, cheetahs, koalas, and hulking gorillas willing to stare you down are among ________ 2,500 creatures at ________ 200-acre zoo, which can be traversed by ________ little train or "zoomobile." In May 1994 ________ new Aquatic and Reptile Center opened. It has ________ 28,000-gallon Pacific Coast marine aquarium, ________ giant octopus, plus ________ robotic sea creatures. 10001 Bluemound Road, (414) 771-3040.

____ **2.** *Milwaukee Public Museum.* ________ impressive interactive rain forest exhibit, ________ life-size roaring dinosaur, ________ Streets of Old Milwaukee, ________ ethnic houses, and ________ major Native American history exhibit are part of ________ city's world-class museum. 800 Wells Sreet, (414) 278-2702 (recorded schedule).

Skyline of Milwaukee, WI.

Source: *The Greater Milwaukee Official Visitors Guide* (1991–92). Published by Plaza Publications, Inc., 1992. Reprinted by permission.

_____ **3.** *Milwaukee Art Museum*. There are more than 20,000 works of _________ fifteenth- to twentieth-century European and American art, with _________ strong contemporary collection that includes Picasso, O'Keeffe, and Warhol; one of _________ world's best Haitian art collections; _________ Frank Lloyd Wright School Collection of Decorative Art and Design, plus _________ temporary exhibits. 750 N. Lincoln Memorial Drive, (414) 224-3200.

_____ **4.** *Milwaukee Brewers* (baseball). See _________ Brewers at _________ Milwaukee County Stadium. For _________ free schedule write _________ team at 201 S. 45th Street, Milwaukee, WI 53214, (414) 933-4114.

_____ **5.** *Badgerland Striders* (running club). _________ Ice Age Trail 50-mile race, _________ Lakefront Marathon, _________ Al McGuire Run, and Storm _________ Bastille Run are among _________ local events. Call (414) 476-7223 for _________ current year's race book.

_____ **6.** *Pabst Theater*. _________ building itself is as significant as _________ performances on its stage. It's one of _________ few remaining structures in _________ United States that date back to _________ Golden Age of _________ German theater in America, which declined at _________ start of _________ World War I. Tours of _________ German Renaissance Revival theater, with terra cotta ornaments and gilded urns, are available. 144 E. Wells, (414) 286-3663.

_____ **7.** *Miller Brewing Co.* Some of _________ brewery's nineteenth-century buildings remain. There are _________ regularly scheduled free tours and tastings. 4000 W. State Street, (414) 931-2000.

_____ **8.** *Schlitz Audubon Center*. Six miles of hiking trails are at __________ 225-acre center. Two paths lead to __________ Lake Michigan. There is __________ "bog walk," __________ mystery pond, and __________ treetop observatory with __________ spectacular view of __________ downtown and __________ lake. 1111 E. Brown Deer Road, (414) 352-2880.

_____ **9.** *Three Brothers Bar and Restaurant*. __________ popular Serbian restaurant since 1958 in one of __________ few remaining corner taverns owned by __________ Schlitz Brewery during __________ late nineteenth- and early twentieth-century. __________ Schlitz globe is on top of __________ turret of __________ landmark building. 2414 S. St. Clair, (414) 481-7530.

From Chris Martell, "Don't Malign Milwaukee,"
Feb. 26, 1995, *Wisconsin State Journal.*

NOTE In lists, for example, phone directories, tourist guides, and maps, *the* is often omitted from proper nouns. Remember to add *the* when needed (e.g., **The** Pabst Theater dates back to **th**e Golden Age of German theater).

Activity 4

Read about Sylvia Ann Hewlett, a woman who had it all in the 1970s: a successful career, marriage, children. Write in the appropriate article, *a/an, the,* or *0,* in the blanks. In some cases, more than one article is possible.

Background. In 1973, Sylvia Hewlett earned ______ (1) Ph.D in economics from ______ (2) Harvard University. After marriage, ______ (3) birth of her first child, Lisa, and six years of teaching at ______ (4) Barnard College, ______ (5) women's college in New York City, ______ (6) dark event forced her to reevaluate her life. In fall 1979, she lost premature twin babies in ______ (7) middle of her **tenure review**. She left ______ (8) Barnard College in 1980 and took ______ (9) job as director of ______ (10) Economic Policy Council, working as ______ (11) economist to **advocate** for families with ______ (12) children. In ______ (13) next decade, she wrote ______ (14) best-selling book, *When* ______ (15) ***Bough*** *Breaks:* ______ (16) *Cost of Neglecting Our Children,* continued to advocate for **policies** beneficial to ______ (17) children, and had two additional children, David and Adam. In 1985, just ______ (18) week before her 40th birthday, Hewlett resigned as director of ______ (19) Council, because it was becoming impossible to both work and take care of her family. In her words, she had become " ______ (20) overburdened, inadequate wife and mother." In 1993, Hewlett founded ______ (21) National Parenting Association, ______ (22) organization committed to creating ______ (23) more family-friendly America.

tenure review the evaluation of a professor's performance for a permanent position at an academic institution
advocate work in support of a particular cause or group
bough tree branch; refers to the well-known nursery rhyme, "Rock-a-bye Baby"
policy a plan, a course of action or a guiding principle

Hewlett reflects on changes in society since ________ (24) 1960s and discusses ________ (25) challenges facing parents today:

In recent years I have devoted much thought to ________ (26) central question: Why is it such ________ (27) hard struggle—this business of being ________ (28) good parent? Why has it become such ________ (29) thankless task—building families and putting children first?

Part of ________ (30) answer lies in our policies. We fail to adequately fund prenatal care or parenting leave. Under our tax code, ________ (31) couple would be better off breeding racehorses than raising ________ (32) children. ________ (33) Most states devote more attention to regulating ________ (34) dog kennels than ________ (35) day-care centers.

Part of ________ (36) answer lies in ________ (37) way our culture has tilted toward ________ (38) self. ________ (39) liberation movements of ________ (40) 1960s greatly increased ________ (41) weight men and women give to self-fulfillment, and this has had tremendous negative effects on ________ (42) children. For, like it or not, there are trade-offs between personal fulfillment and family well-being. Creating ________ (43) home and raising ________ (44) children are time-intensive activities that claim large amounts of adult energy in ________ (45) prime of life—energy that cannot then be spent on advancing ________ (46) career—or working out at ________ (47) gym—for that matter.

All of which is not ________ (48) long-winded way of recommending that we return to ________ (49) traditional world of ________ (50) 1950s. Women are no longer able to take ________ (51) entire responsibility for ________ (52) family life. Husbands and fathers, employers and government, all have to pull their weight in this business of nurturing.

From Sylvia Ann Hewlett, "Tough Choices, Great Rewards,"
Parade, July 17, 1994. Reprinted with permission from *Parade,* © 1994.

Activity 5

Groups. The following topic sentences begin the three remaining paragraphs from the article cited in Activity 4. In groups of three, have each person choose one of the topic sentences and write a paragraph, showing how (1) husbands and fathers, (2) corporations, and (3) government can contribute to raising a family. When you're finished, exchange paragraphs and comment on each other's ideas and use of articles.

LEARNING STRATEGY

Personalizing: Using examples from your own country and culture is okay if you don't know much about a topic in another country.

1. Take husbands and fathers. Right now only 1 percent of fathers take paternity leave (time off when a child is born or adopted).
2. Corporations can, in fact, do many things to give parents the "gift of time."
3. Government also has a powerful role to play.

LEARNING STRATEGY

Managing Your Learning: Focusing on getting your ideas on paper first and checking your grammar later will help you both think and write.

Activity 6

Have you ever been in a position of having to choose between school and family or between work and family? If you have, describe in about a page your situation and what you did. If you have never made such a choice, imagine a situation in which you must and describe what you think you would do. Pay special attention to your ideas and to your use of articles in your paper.

Language in Context: Sentences

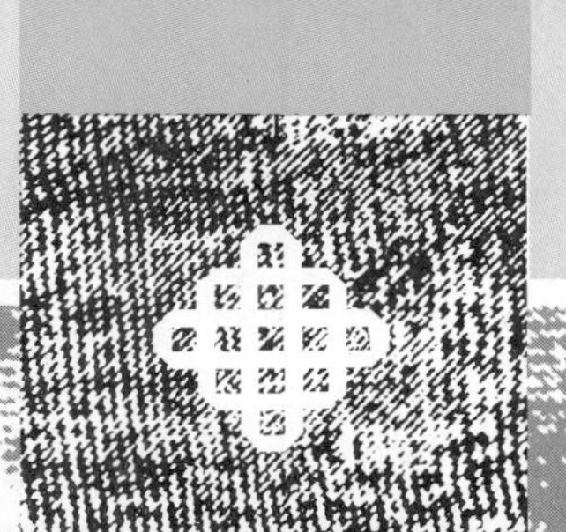

Lesson 18: Parallel Structure

Words, Phrases, and Clauses

PREVIEW

With a partner or your class, do the following:

1. Define the word *anniversary*.

____

____

____

2. Complete a semantic web for *anniversary.* (Beginning with the word *anniversary,* think of related words and concepts that branch out from the center like a spider's web.)

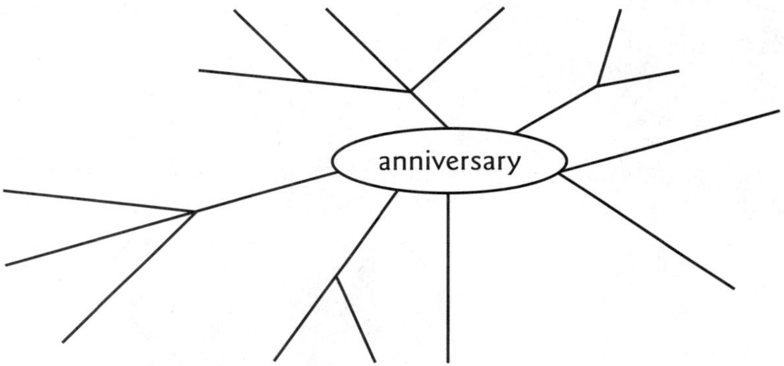

3. Read the following passage about a World War II anniversary.

While most of the world slept and a few anxiously waited, 23,000 Allied **paratroopers** took off from England to land behind the German line in Normandy, France. They were followed by six battleships, 22 cruisers, and 93 detroyers. By 6:30 A.M. on June 6, 1944, thousands of **Allied infantrymen** began to land on the beaches of Normandy, code-named Utah, Omaha, Gold, Juno, and Sword. So began the turning point in the war against Germany: D-day.

paratroopers foot soldiers (infantry) trained to parachute

Allied infantrymen foot soldiers from nations (primarily Great Britain, Russia, and the United States) united against the Axis powers (primarily Germany, Italy, and later, Japan)

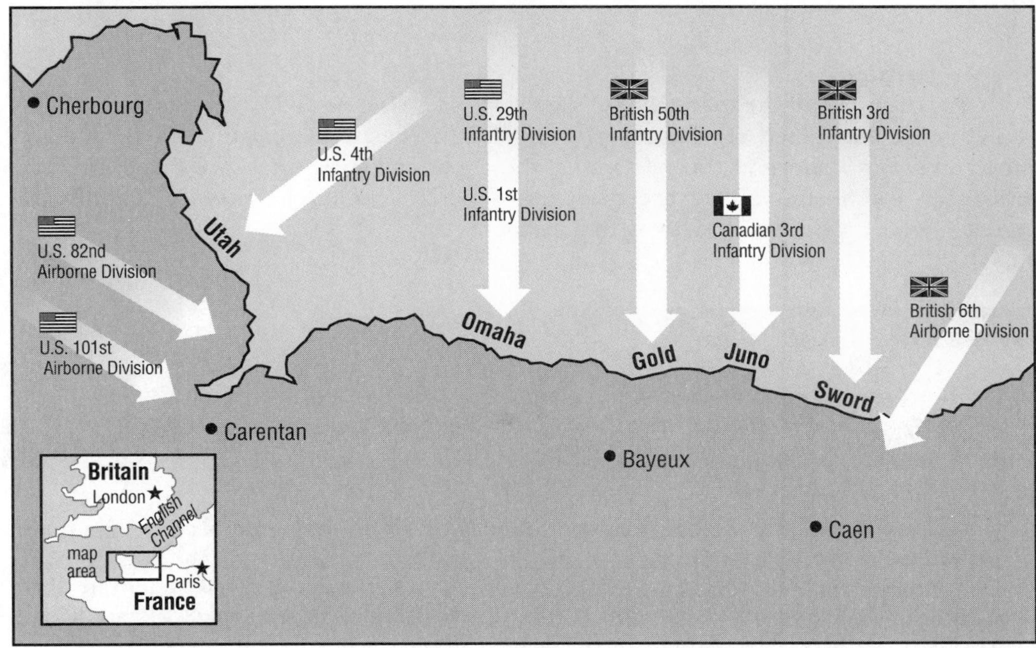

PRESENTATION

The underlined words, phrases, and clauses in the Preview are examples of lists of two or more items. The items in each list follow **parallel structure**; in other words, each item in a list is the same kind of structure: all clauses, all phrases, or all nouns. The use of parallel structure is not just for formal writing or memorable speeches. It can also help make any writer's or speaker's ideas clear and focused. Compare these two sentences:

1. I have full confidence in your courage, devotion to duty and skill in battle. (Gen. Dwight D. Eisenhower, Supreme Allied Commander, to his troops upon the invasion of Normandy, June 6, 1944)
2. I have full confidence in your courage, devotion to duty and how well you fight.

In sentence 2, "how well you fight" is out of place in a list that begins with noun phrases. It clearly distracts from the author's ideas.

Punctuating lists. Using correct punctuation with lists that follow parallel structure contributes to clarity and style in speech and writing. In English, lists of two items do *not* contain commas, but lists of three or more items have commas between them:

- Your task will not be an easy one. Your enemy is well trained, well equipped, and battle hardened. (General Eisenhower)

In British English, there is no comma before the coordinator in a list of three or more items. But in American English, many teachers require it. For rules about punctuating lists with different structures, see *The Tapestry Grammar,* Chapter 14, pages 333–334.

PRACTICE

Activity 1

Partners. Read the following passage from an article on D-day. Examples of parallel structure are underlined. How many *different* structures are underlined? Circle the kinds of structures that appear in the passage in the three categories that are listed after the passage. If you need to review these structures, see *The Tapestry Grammar,* Chapter 14, pages 333–334. Check your work with a partner.

LEARNING STRATEGY

Overcoming Limitations: Understanding every word in a second language is not always necessary to complete a task.

(1)Fifty years later, veterans of the Allied forces who defeated Nazi Germany are invading Normandy again to gaze at the beaches they stormed, walk the sunken roads they fought over, mourn at the military cemeteries, but most of all, celebrate their triumph. (2)On the next big anniversary 10 years hence, most of these old soldiers—and many of those who lived through the cataclysm of World War II—will be gone.

(3)Presidents and generals and ordinary folk will come to pay homage in Europe this week, to remember a great battle in a good cause. (4)"That war," [President] Clinton told the graduating class at the U.S. Naval Academy last week, "marked the turning point of our century, when we joined with our Allies to stem a dark tide of dictatorship and to start a flow of democracy and freedom that continues to sweep the world."

Excerpted from Bruce W. Nelan, "Ike's Invasion," *Time,* June 6, 1994.

WORDS	PHRASES	CLAUSES
Nouns	Noun phrases	Independent clauses
Verbs	Prepositional phrases	Subordinate clauses
Adjectives	Verbal phrases	(e.g., *wh*-clauses,
	Predicates	adverbial clauses)

Activity 2

Read the following passage from a man who fought on D-Day. Underline words that are examples of parallel structure in the passage. How many *different* structures did you find? Circle the structures in the three categories that are listed after the passage.

DAN DARLING, 73, CANADIAN

(He landed at Juno Beach with Canada's Stormont, Dundas, and Glengarry Highlanders. Their mission was to race 10 miles to Caen's airport on fold-up bicycles.)

(1)"Going over, the officers read a message from Ike [Eisenhower's nickname]. (2)One of the guys prayed and then joked that this time he really meant it. (3)I don't think I was ever afraid. (4)You were betting on coming back."

(5)"The first sight of France was the smoke, then the fires on the beach. (6)There was so much happening: shells whistling in, buildings burning, aircraft overhead, Jerry [German soldiers] letting go with 88-mm guns. (7)We all grabbed our bicycles, and I remember the water under my chin. (8)I had 78 lb. of gear, not counting the bike and steel helmet. (9)There were bodies in the water, and bodies lined up under blankets on the shore."

(10)"On the beach, there was no standing around. We tried using the fold-up bikes we'd trained on for two years. (11)But the rubble on the roads made the whole thing impractical. (12)After about three miles, we were ordered to stack them up in a heap. (13)We dug slit trenches the first night in a churchyard; Jerry was maybe 1,000 yards away. (14)When we tried to negotiate with a local farmer to buy some eggs, he was mystified by our Quebec French and finally asked in English, 'What do you want?' (15)He had been a steward on the French liner *Normandie* and lived for years in New York. (16)He gave us 15 eggs and green onions; so we made an omelet."

(17)"Once we got inland, Jerry turned out to be mostly fanatical Hitler Youth and conscripts from Italy, Poland, and Austria. (18)The one who shot me was so young he'd never needed to shave. (19)You couldn't think about getting killed: either you got them, or they got you."

Excerpted from Bruce W. Nelan, "Men Who Fought," *Time,* June 6, 1994.

WORDS	**PHRASES**	**CLAUSES**
Nouns	Noun phrases	Independent clauses
Verbs	Prepositional phrases	Subordinate clauses
Adjectives	Verbal phrases	(e.g., *wh*-clauses,
	Predicates	adverbial clauses)

Activity 3

The following pairs of sentences are adapted from a short course on D-day for people too young to remember it.* Combine each pair of sentences into one sentence, using parallel structures with coordinators (*and, but*) or *not*. The first two are done as examples.

1. The real name for the Allied invasion of Normandy's beaches was not "D-day."
   The real name of the Allied invasion of Normandy's beaches was "Operation Overlord."

   The real name for the Allied invasion of Normandy beaches was not "D-day" but "Operation Overlord."

2. The Allies tried to fool Hitler into thinking their invasion would occur at Pas de Calais by sending false intelligence information.
   The Allies tried to fool Hitler into thinking their invasion would occur at Pas de Calais by beginning a fake invasion there on June 5, 1944.

   The Allies tried to fool Hitler into thinking their invasion would occur at Pas de Calais by sending false intelligence information and beginning a fake invasion there on June 5, 1944.

3. Gen. George Marshall was President Roosevelt's first choice as commander of the Allied invasion.
   Gen. Dwight D. Eisenhower was not President Roosevelt's first choice as commander of the Allied invasion.

   ____

   ____

   ____

*Adapted from Christine Crumbo, "20-Something Important D-Day Facts," *Wisconsin State Journal,* June 5, 1994. Knight-Ridder Newspapers.

4. The D-day invasion force was the largest in history, with 4,000 ships and 600 warships.
The D-day invasion force was the largest in history with 10,000 planes.

___

___

___

5. American troops took the westernmost beaches of Normandy, code-named Utah and Omaha.
British troops took the easternmost beaches of Normandy, code-named Gold and Sword.

___

___

___

6. In a cemetery at St. James, France, 4,329 crosses mark the graves of Americans who died in the D-day invasion.
In a cemetery at St. James, France, 81 Stars of David mark the graves of Americans who died in the D-day invasion.

___

___

___

7. Some famous pictures of the invasion were taken by *Life* magazine photographer John Capa, who survived Normandy.
Some famous pictures of the invasion were taken by *Life* magazine photographer John Capa, who died documenting another war, Vietnam.

___

___

___

___

8. If you like to read, history professor John Dreifort recommends *Six Armies in Normandy* by historian John Keegan.
If you want to know more about D-day, history professor John Dreifort recommends *Six Armies in Normandy* by historian John Keegan.

___

___

___

___

Activity 4

Read these sentences from student essays on *freedom.* Correct the problems with parallelism in these sentences. There may be more than one way to correct the sentences.

1. Freedom is when you be old enough, when you are on your own, when you leave your parents.
2. Freedom means many things to me: to do anything we want and go wherever we want, not controlled by others, not held back by fear or distrust.
3. Freedom is to believe in your own thoughts and what you say.
4. Also you have to have responsibility for what you do and what you going to do in the future.

5. When I was in Mexico, I could do anything I wanted, like go to dances, fishing, parties.
6. Freedom is a word that makes everybody happy and when race, color, and religion don't matter.

Activity 5

Think of an important anniversary in your life or an occasion you like to remember, such as past holidays, vacations, learning experiences, or important "firsts" in your life: your first day at school, your first time away from home, your first day at a job. Refer to the semantic web you created in the Preview for additional ideas. Complete the following phrases by adding information in lists of two or more items. Pay attention to how the phrase ends as a clue to the kind of parallel structure to use. This activity isn't a composition but a way to generate possible ideas for one.

1. On [give date], I was doing several things:
____
____
____
2. I was feeling [adjectives] ______________________________
____
3. I tried to ______________________________
____
____
4. All around me, people [or another subject] were ______________________________
____
____
5. It was then that I noticed/decided/realized that ______________________________
____
____
6. The only thing I could do was ______________________________
____
____
7. In the end I learned ______________________________
____
____

LEARNING STRATEGY

Managing Your Learning: Using a new structure selectively helps create variety in speech and writing.

Activity 6

Individuals/Partners. Write up your memories of an important event in your life from Activity 5 and include some of the lists you generated. Share your paper with a partner and comment on each other's ideas and use of parallel structure.

Lesson 19: Ties within Sentences

Coordinators and Subordinators

PREVIEW

Ask yourself these questions and then discuss your answers with a partner.

1. What do these dates have in common?
   October 4, 1957; April 12, 1961; January 27, 1967; July 20, 1969; November 14, 1969; January 31, 1971; July 26, 1971; April 16, 1972; December 7, 1972.
2. Which date marks the 25th anniversary of the first humans to walk on the moon? (It's okay to guess.)
3. Read this passage on space exploration.

ONE SMALL STEP . . . ONE GIANT LEAP

(1)On October 4, 1957, the Soviets launched the first rocket into space, <u>and</u> four months later, the Americans succeeded in launching one, too. (2)On April 12, 1961, the Soviets launched another rocket, <u>and</u> Yuri Gagarin became the first human to orbit the earth. (3)Within a month, Alan Shepard became the first American to fly in space, <u>but</u> his 15-minute trip took him only a few hundred miles over the Atlantic Ocean. (4)Then on July 20, 1969, Neil Armstrong and Buzz Aldrin took their historic first steps on the moon. (5)<u>Yet</u> their success was not without cost. (6)Two and a half years earlier, on January 27, 1967, three U.S. astronauts died in their Apollo capsule in a preflight test. (7)The total cost of the venture, including five later moon landings, was about $30 billion, <u>or</u> about $100 billion in today's dollars.

Based on Mark Carreau, "25 Years since Historic Landing," *Wisconsin State Journal,* July 17, 1994. *Houston Chronicle.*

PRESENTATION

The underlined words in the Preview passage are examples of **coordinators** (coordinating conjunctions). They are words that can be used to combine independent clauses. (In the passage, *or* combines prepositional phrases rather than clauses.) There are seven basic coordinators in English: ***for, and, nor, but, or, yet, so***. A simple way to remember these seven is with the acronym FANBOYS, which stands for the first letter of each coordinator. Table 5.1 summarizes the meaning and use of these coordinators.

LEARNING STRATEGY

Remembering New Material: Making a word out of the first letters (an *acronym*) helps you remember related vocabulary.

TABLE 5.1 The Seven Basic Coordinators

MEANING	GENERAL USE (formal and informal)	FORMAL USE
Adding	and	
Contrasting	but	yet
Concluding/stating a reason	so	for
Giving alternatives	or	nor

Punctuating with coordinators. There is only one rule for punctuating two independent clauses combined with a coordinator: add a comma before the coordinator.

CORRECT

- President John F. Kennedy set the goal to land on the moon before 1970, but Vice President Lyndon B. Johnson was largely responsible for carrying it out.

INCORRECT (**run-on sentence**)

- President John F. Kennedy set the goal to land on the moon before 1970 but Vice President Lyndon B. Johnson was largely responsible for carrying it out.

INCORRECT (**comma splice**)

- President John F. Kennedy set the goal to land on the moon before 1970, Vice President Lyndon B. Johnson was largely responsible for carrying it out.

The easiest way to correct a run-on sentence is to add a comma before the coordinator. For three ways to correct a comma splice, see Table 5.2.

TABLE 5.2 Correcting Comma Splices

WAYS TO CORRECT COMMA SPLICES	PATTERN SP = Subject + Predicate	USE
Substitute a period for the comma. Begin a new sentence with a capital letter	SP. SP.	Used in all writing
Add a coordinator (+) after the comma (except between two very short clauses)	SP, + SP.	Used in all writing
Substitute a semicolon (;) for the coma (when two sentences are clearly related).	SP; SP.	Used in formal writing

PRACTICE

Activity 1

Read some responses to the question, "Where were you when Apollo II astronauts first walked on the moon?" (9:56 P.M. CDT, July 20, 1969). The responses have errors in punctuation. Correct the errors.

1. We were at a barbecue picnic at a friend's house, then someone called out that Apollo 11 was about to land.
2. I was working as a waitress at a country club so I had to see the landing on the news later.
3. I was at a friend's house and we were watching the whole thing on TV.
4. I can't remember what we were doing, I think we were driving to New York or something.
5. I wasn't even born yet but if I had been, I would have been watching TV.
6. We were camping in Colorado so I missed the big moment.
7. We were at the Dairy Queen eating ice cream or maybe we were already home.
8. We were in Mission Control Center in Houston all of us were glued to our display screens.

FOR YOUR INFORMATION Dairy Queen is a U.S. chain of fast-food restaurants that specializes in ice cream and other dairy products.

Activity 2

Read about adverbial **subordinators** and then complete the activity that follows.

Writers regularly combine independent clauses with subordinate clauses, which begin with **subordinators** (subordinating conjunctions). Subordinators show how subordinate (adverbial) clauses are related in meaning to independent clauses. Table 5.3 lists common subordinators for adverbial clauses.

TABLE 5.3 Adverbial Subordinators

after	in case	whatever
although	in order that	when
as	no matter what	whenever
as if	now that	where
as . . . as	once	wherever
as though	since	whereas
because	so that	whether . . . or not
before	though	whichever
even though	unless	while
if, even if	until	whoever

Some coordinators are related in meaning to subordinators, as Table 5.4 shows.

TABLE 5.4 Coordinators and Subordinators with Similar Meanings

MEANING	COORDINATORS	SUBORDINATORS
Contrasting	but yet	although even though though
Concluding/stating a reason	so for	because since

Punctuating adverbial clauses. If the adverbial clause occurs *before* an independent clause, it is followed by a comma, as in (1) below. If it occurs *after* an independent clause, there is usually no comma between the two clauses, as in (2). When a very long adverbial clause occurs after an independent clause, there may be a comma before it.

CORRECT

1. Although the first lunar landing on July 20, 1969, is the most famous, there were actually six lunar landings in the Apollo program.
2. There were actually six lunar landings in the Apollo program although the first lunar landing on July 20, 1969, is the most famous.

Sentences (3) and (4) illustrate two common problems with adverbial clauses.

INCORRECT

3. Although the first lunar landing on July 20, 1969, is the most famous, but there were actually six lunar landings in the Apollo program. (CORRECTION: Use *although* or *but,* not both.)
4. There were actually six lunar landings in the Apollo program. Although the first lunar landing on July 20, 1969, is the most famous. (CORRECTION: Connect the subordinate clause beginning with *although* to the independent clause, omit the period, and change the capital letter *A* to lowercase *a.*)

Rewrite sentences (3) and (4) correctly as (5) and (6).

5. ____

____

6. ____

____

Activity 3

Write example sentences on any topic using the following subordinators. Vary the position of the adverbial clause so that it sometimes occurs at the beginning and sometimes at the end of the sentence. Remember to punctuate correctly. One is done for you as an example.

SUBORDINATOR	EXAMPLE
1. although	
2. even though	
3. though*	
4. while*	*While your answer is correct, it doesn't answer the question completely.*

*More formal

NOTE *Though* can also occur by itself at the end of a sentence to show contrast:
She likes math. She doesn't like accounting, *though*.

Activity 4

Partners. Write example sentences using the following subordinators. Vary the position of the adverbial clause in your sentences and answer the question at the end. Share your sentences with a partner and make any changes needed to correct them.

SUBORDINATOR	EXAMPLE
1. Time	
a. after	
b. as soon as	*Call me as soon as you know the answer.*
c. before	
d. once	
e. since	
f. until	
g. when	
h. whenever	
i. while	
2. Place	
where	*Where she went, I'll never know.*

Activity 5

Write example sentences using the following subordinators. Vary the position of the adverbial clause so that it sometimes occurs at the beginning and sometimes at the end of the sentence.

SUBORDINATOR	EXAMPLE
1. because	
2. since	
3. now that*	*Now that you're here, he's not coming.*
4. as long as	

*Informal

Activity 6

Partners. Review Table 5.4 on page 116 before you begin. Then, in the following sentences, replace the underlined coordinators with subordinators and the underlined subordinators with coordinators. To keep the meaning of the sentences the same, change the punctuation and word order as needed. Check your work with a partner.

1. <u>Even though</u> President Kennedy was convinced the United States could send someone to the moon by 1970, some of his top scientific experts doubted it.

   ____

   ____

2. Some people thought Kennedy's May 1961 announcement to land on the moon was a bold decision, <u>yet</u> others thought it was an attempt to distract the public from troubles in Cuba (the unsuccessful Bay of Pigs invasion on April 17, 1961).

   ____

   ____

   ____

3. President Kennedy celebrated the earlier space rides of astronauts Alan Shepard and John Glenn <u>because</u> he could unite the country around the space race.

   ____

   ____

4. Some argue that President Eisenhower's interstate highway system has had more impact on people than the moon landing, <u>but</u> others disagree.

   ____

   ____

5. <u>Since</u> the United States succeeded in putting a man on the moon, some people wonder why America hasn't succeeded in more earthly social programs, such as health care reform.

   ____

   ____

   ____

Activity 7

Partners. Review Table 5.3 on page 116 before you begin. Replace the underlined subordinators in the following sentences with another subordinator from the table, keeping the meaning of the sentence the same. In some sentences, you may need to make other small changes in wording. More than one answer may be possible. Check your work with a partner.

1. <u>As</u> Neil Armstrong set foot on the moon on July 20, 1969, he announced, "That's one small step for man. One giant leap for mankind."
2. <u>Now that</u> the Cold War tensions between the United States and the former Soviet Union are gone, a global alliance is developing in order to build an international space station by 2002.
3. A manned space station is needed <u>so that</u> the nations involved learn how to operate in space with people.
4. <u>After</u> the space station is built, scientists plan to operate it for 10 to 15 years.
5. <u>Once</u> the United States and its partners build a space station and learn how to support human life there, they can begin to establish a moon base for further explorations.
6. According to some experts, <u>unless</u> these nations go beyond a space station to build a lunar base, their efforts and money will be wasted.

Adapted from Mark Carreau, "When Will Humans Return," *Wisconsin State Journal,* July 17, 1994. *Houston Chronicle.*

Lesson 20: Ties within Sentences

Pronouns in Affirmative and Negative Sentences

PREVIEW

1. **Think**
   - **a.** What's the difference between an *invention* and a *discovery*?

     ___

     ___

   - **b.** Think of an invention *and* a discovery that have made people's lives easier, safer, or healthier.

     Invention: ___

     Discovery: ___

2. **Pair** Compare your answers to (a) and (b) with a partner.
3. **Share**
   - **a.** Write everyone's answers on a blackboard, a transparency, or large sheets of paper. Record this information for a later activity.
   - **b.** Answer these questions with "yes" or "no."
     - Did anyone choose the telephone?
     - Did anybody choose the automobile (car)?
     - Did anybody choose television?
     - Did anyone choose electricity?

PRESENTATION

The underlined words in (3) in the Preview are examples of compound pronouns. (In 3a, everyone's functions as a possessive.) The meaning of a compound pronoun depends on the quantifier it is related to. Table 5.5 lists the compound pronouns and their related quantifiers.

TABLE 5.5 Compound Pronouns and Related Quantifiers

QUANTIFIER	COMPOUND PRONOUN (for people)	COMPOUND PRONOUN (for things)	USE
every	everyone everybody	everything	to make positive (affirmative) statements that include all
any	anyone anybody	anything	to ask questions or make negative statements
some	someone somebody	something	to make positive (affirmative) statements
no	no one nobody	nothing	to make negative statements

1. Affirmative
   - Question: Did anybody choose the telephone?
   - Statement: Everybody did. (= all people)
     Somebody did. (= at least one person)
2. Negative
   - Question: Didn't anybody choose the telephone?
     (implies an element of surprise or disbelief in the question)
   - Statement: I don't think anybody did.
     Nobody did. (= not one person, not *any* + body)

PRACTICE

Activity 1

Refer to your class list of inventions and discoveries from the Preview, or ask at least five people to name an important invention *and* a discovery. Answer the following questions, first by circling *Yes* or *No* and an appropriate compound pronoun and then by writing the answer in the same way.

1. Did anyone choose the telephone?

   (Yes/No); (everyone/someone/no one) did.
2. Did anybody choose the automobile (car)?

   (Yes/No); (everybody/somebody/nobody) did.
3. Did anybody choose television?

   (Yes/No); (everybody/somebody/nobody) did.
4. Did anyone choose electricity?

   (Yes/No); (everyone/someone/no one) did.
5. Did anybody choose penicillin?

   (Yes/No); (everybody/somebody/nobody) did.

Answer the questions in the same way.

1. Did anybody choose the computer?

   ____
2. Did anyone choose the atom?

   ____
3. Did anybody choose X rays?

   ____
4. Did anyone choose plastic?

   ____
5. Did anyone choose the zipper?

   ____

Activity 2

Partners. Look over Table 5.6 on inventions and discoveries. Write five questions to ask your partner, similar to the following:

- Could people eat chocolate bars before 1760?
- Could anyone drink Coca-Cola in 1890?

When appropriate, use **no one/nobody, some + noun, someone/somebody,** or **everyone/everybody** in your answers e.g., "No, **no one** could," or "Yes, **some people** could."

To make the activity more challenging, don't look at the table when you answer your partner's questions.

TABLE 5.6 Selected Inventions and Discoveries

INVENTION/DISCOVERY	INVENTOR/DISCOVERER	YEAR
telescope	Sir Isaac Newton (England)	1672
chocolate bar	Francois-Loyis Cailler (France)	1762
sandwich	John Montagu, Fourth Earl of Sandwich (England)	1762
Coca-Cola	Dr. John S. Permberton (U.S.)	1886
viruses	Dmitry Ivanovsky (Russia)	1892
zipper	Whitcomb Judson (U.S.)	1893
electric washing machine	Alva J. Fisher (U.S.)	1901
gene	Wilhelm Johannsen (Denmark), the name;	1909
	Thomas Hunt Morgan (U.S.), the theory	1910
PVC (plastic, or polyvinylchloride)	Professor Klatte (Germany)	1913
Pluto (the planet)	Clyde Tombaugh (U.S.)	1930
microwave oven	Percy Le Baron Spencer (U.S.)	1945
nonstick pan	Marc Gregoire (France)	1954

Activity 3

Groups. Think back to a recent event at which you received gifts (birthday, Christmas, another holiday, or another event). On a separate piece of paper, do the following:

1. Write your name on the paper.
2. List **everything** you received (include any monetary gifts).
3. List **something** you received that you didn't really need.
4. Did you return or give **anything** away because you didn't like it or need it? If so, list those item(s).
5. Exchange papers with everyone in your group. Circle and write your name above any items in response to (3) or (4) that you would like or need.
6. When you get your paper back, summarize who wanted what item(s), using some of the following quantifiers/compound pronouns: **no one/nobody**, **nothing**, **a couple, a few**, **some**, (almost) **everyone/everybody**, **everything**, **any**, **anything**. Your teacher may want you to do this orally or in writing.

Activity 4

All compound pronouns are grammatically singular. However, in casual speech and writing, English speakers often use *they/them/their* to refer to *everyone/everybody, someone/somebody, anyone/anybody,* and *no one/nobody* to avoid using the singular forms *he/him/his* or *she/her/her* for both males and females:

- Everybody should write their answers on a piece of paper.

In formal speech and writing, the singular pronoun forms are preferred, or you can avoid the problem altogether by rewording:

- You should write your answers on a piece of paper.
- All students should write their answers on a piece of paper.

See *The Tapestry Grammar,* Chapter 7, pages 167–169, for other examples.

Rewrite the following sentences to avoid the problem of number agreement with compound pronouns and other pronoun forms.

1. When somebody thinks of the origin of the automobile, they usually think of Henry Ford.
2. However, if someone checks an encyclopedia, they will find that two brothers, Charles and Frank Duryea, produced the first gasoline-powered automobile in 1893, the "buggyaut."
3. Anybody who bought their first car in the United States between 1908 and 1927 had a better chance of buying a Model T Ford than a buggyaut, though, since 15 million were produced.
4. During those years, everybody who owned a Model T was writing to Henry Ford; their letters sometimes totaled 5,000 a week.
5. To anyone who wanted to make their fortune selling Ford cars, the *Ford Times* had this advice: "Early to bed and early to rise. Work like hell and advertise."
6. After 1914, when Ford began to share profits with Ford Motor Company workers, everyone who worked for the motor company loved their boss.

Based on National Geographic Society, *Inventors and Discoveries: Changing Our World.* Washington, DC: National Geographic Society, 1988.

6

CHAPTER

Language in Context: Discourse

Lesson 21: Ties across Sentences

Articles, Other Determiners and Pronouns

PREVIEW

Have you ever been stuck in traffic that wasn't moving? Soon you may be able to avoid the problem completely with Prometheus.

(1) The Prometheus system was launched in 1986 and is the most ambitious of all the in-car computer-guided driving systems currently being developed. (2) A joint European effort, the goal of Prometheus is to reduce the problems of **traffic congestion,** pollution, and safety. (3) Three models are in development, including one system that could see through fog using a special camera and project road conditions ahead onto the **windshield.** (4) A computer would determine whether the car was moving safely and would automatically slow it down if it believed the situation to be dangerous. (5) Another system uses an **on-board computer** that connects into a city's traffic patterns. (6) This system would tell the driver which roads were crowded, where parking is available, and even which hotels had **vacancies.** (7) Some of these devices could be ready by 1995, but Prometheus is not expected to be fully operational until the next century.

Slightly adapted from Valérie-Ann Giscard d'Estaing and Mark Young (Eds.), "The Prometheus System," in *Inventions and Discoveries 1993,* New York: Facts on File.

traffic congestion too many cars on the road; overcrowded street
windshield transparent glass in the front of a car that protects the driver and passengers from the wind
on-board computer a computer inside a car
vacancy available room

PRESENTATION

The underlined words in the Preview are all examples of words that create ties across sentences, such as articles, other determiners (e.g., quantifiers, *this/that, another/the other/other*), and pronouns. When these ties are clear, they make speech and writing easier to understand. When they are unclear or ambiguous, they interfere with understanding.

One potential source of unclear ties is confusion between the pronoun *it* and the demonstratives *this/that*. Table 6.1 summarizes some important differences between these words.

TABLE 6.1 Distinguishing between *it* and *this/that*

USE		EXAMPLE
Specific *it* *this/that*	refers to specific things in singular noun phrases	**The microwave oven** was invented in 1945. **It/This** is an essential appliance in millions of homes today.
General *it* *this/that*	refers to a previous idea—a verbal phrase, clause, sentence, or paragraph	The only problem with microwave ovens is **that there is no standard way to operate them.** **This** is confusing for some people. **It** is frustrating for others.
Empty *it*	fills the subject position when there is no real subject	**It** is important *not* to use metal containers in a microwave oven.

PRACTICE

Activity 1

Have you ever tried to find good tomatoes in the winter? There may be hope in the future with FLAVR SAVR. In the following passage, the underlined words all refer to earlier words, phrases, or ideas (the referent). Some of these ties are within sentences and others are between sentences. For each of the underlined words, draw an arrow to the referent and circle it. One is done as an example.

A FLAVOR SAVER FOR TOMATOES

(1) Most tomatoes sold in stores are picked while they are still green and ripen on their way to the store. (2) However, consumers often complain that the flavor is not as good as that of fresh-picked tomatoes. (3) Recognizing this problem, the American company Calgene has patented the PG Gene (commercial trademark FLAVR SAVR), which is the critical ingredient in producing a genetically **enhanced** tomato that can be picked ripe and can last for two weeks before rotting. (4) These genetically engineered tomatoes, it is claimed, keep their flavor when they reach the consumer. (5) This happens because the PG **enzyme suppresses** the enzyme that results in fruit softening. (6) This type of biotechnology research is being applied by many companies to other fruits and vegetables such as carrots, celery, and peppers.

Slightly adapted from Valérie-Anne Giscard d'Estaing and Marc Younc, (Eds.), "Antisense Polygalacturonase (PG) Gene," in *Inventions and Discoveries 1993*. New York: Facts on File.

enhanced improved
enzyme a type of protein produced by living organisms that sets off a particular biochemical response
suppress to hold back, prevent something from happening

Activity 2

There are two other occurrences of *that* and *it* in the passage in Activity 1 that do *not* refer to earlier referents. Put a box around these words in the passage and identify their grammatical use. You may want to review Table 5.1 and Activity 3 in Lesson 16 to review uses of *that* and *it* first.

1. ______________________________
2. ______________________________

Activity 3

Using articles in discourse. Most nouns are marked with an indefinite article when they are mentioned for the first time because they are nonspecific: their identity is not known to the listener or reader. In later sentences, the same noun is marked with the definite article because it is specific: both the speaker/writer and listener/reader know what the noun refers to. Nouns are made specific by

1. Repetition when the noun is repeated:
   - There is an important historical landmark in the bustling Ginza district of Tokyo, the Hattori clock tower.
   - The landmark survived the firebombing of World War II.
2. Indirect reference when the noun is not repeated but the context makes the reference clear:
   - The 1950s and 1960s was the period of Japan's most rapid growth.
   - But at the time, the country was modest and tentative about its future.

Read about a more recent landmark in the Ginza district that has been famous as a "global trendsetter" since the 1960s. In the following passage, articles are omitted. Add articles (*the, a/an*) as needed in the blanks. Remember that unique nouns are specific without prior mention and require a definite article (see Activity 4 in this lesson).

(1)_______ Sony Building was built to promote (2)_______ vision of Sony as a "lifestyle superpower." All rectangles and clean lines, (3)_______ eight-story tower is (4)_______ Bauhaus-like reflection of (5)_______ highly polished design of Sony products. (6)_______ building "was designed to be like Sony from (7)_______ outside, and from (8)_______ inside," says company spokesman Hiroshi Takahashi.

(9)_______ entire exterior wall was fitted with 2,268 12-inch television picture tubes, creating (10)_______ synchronized display of Sony technological power. (11)"_______ new landmark in Ginza at night," (12)_______ daily *Yomiuri Shimbun* declared in (13)_______ article written during (14)_______ building's dedication in 1966. (15)_______ building became Sony's showcase. (16)_______ first Trinitron television set was rolled out here, as was (17)_______ first Sony Walkman® and (18)_______ company's first high-definition television. More than 15,000 visitors daily still flow past (19)_______ ever-changing product displays on (20)_______ spiraling staircase. Its theater, its helpful assistants, and its basement shop have made (21)_______ Sony Building (22)_______ must-stop for visitors in Japan.

Adapted from Craig Forman, "Totem in Tokyo" [Special Section: War's End], *Wall Street Journal,* Apirl 24, 1995.

Activity 4

Recognizing unique nouns. Unique nouns are understood to be specific without prior mention and require a definite article. A noun is unique because

1. There is only one in the world (the sun, the moon).
2. It can be identified in a specific context:
   We were waiting in line to buy books. The cashier was punching in prices as fast as she could. The store manager opened up another line. (There was only one cashier and one store manager.)
3. It can be identified by a modifier:
   a. *Postmodifiers* (prepositional phrases, *wh*-clauses, verbal phrases):
   We were waiting in line to buy books. The person in front of me was getting more and more impatient. The people listening to their Walkmans® looked bored.
   b. *Some determiners* (ordinal numbers) and *premodifiers* (superlative adjectives):
   The second person in line was using his checkbook as a fan because it was the hottest day of the year.
4. It was mentioned before:
   The woman behind me was opening her backpack. She was looking for her credit card in one of the pockets (of the backpack).
5. It is a proper noun that requires *the* (Chapter 4, Lesson 14).

Read the following sentences and explain why the underlined nouns are unique. Write the number of the reason above the noun.

1. If you've had it with the quality of television programming you're watching, then the latest invention of William Johnson is for you.
2. It's the **Tantrum** brick; you pick it up, throw it at the TV set, and, presto, the TV switches itself off.

3. There is no damage to the screen because the brick is made of foam.
4. A micro-transmitter inside the brick transmits a message to the receiver (in this case the TV set), which picks up the signal.

Slightly adapted from Valérie-Anne Giscard d'Estaing and Marc Young, (Eds.), "The Tantrum Brick," in *Inventions and Discoveries 1993*. New York: Facts on File, 1993.

tantrum a sudden show of bad temper

Activity 5

Using pronouns clearly (Partners). When you speak or write, the referent for any pronoun should be clear so that listeners or readers link the pronoun to the word(s) it refers to. A pronoun usually refers to the first thing or idea that agrees with it in number and/or gender:

- William Johnson's latest invention is the Tantrum brick. You pick it up, throw it at the TV set and presto, the TV switches itself off.

Two problems to avoid with pronoun reference are:

1. Confusing pronoun reference. The same pronoun refers to two different things: A computer determines whether the car is moving safely and automatically slows it down if it believes the situation to be dangerous.
2. Ambiguous pronoun reference. One pronoun can refer to two or more things: The first Trinitron television set was on display at the Sony Building, as were the first Walkman® and the company's first high-definition television. This caused a big sensation with the public. (*This* could refer to one of the inventions being displayed or all three.)

Some of the following sentences about the invention of Post-it® notes contain examples of faulty pronoun reference. These problems are underlined. Read the passage and then make changes to correct the problems. Discuss your changes with a partner.

(1) In 1974 Art Fry was employed by the 3M company in product development. (2) On Sundays they sang in the choir of North Presbyterian Church in North St. Paul, Minnesota. (3) He marked his choir book with **scraps** of paper to help him find the proper music quickly at the proper time. (4) But sometimes it fell out without warning, causing him to page through the music in a panic in the second service.

(5) "I don't know if it was a dull sermon or divine inspiration," says Fry, "but my mind began to wander and suddenly I thought of an **adhesive** that had been discovered several years earlier by another 3M scientist, Dr. Spencer Silver." (6) Spencer had **discarded** the adhesive, Fry remembered, because they were not strong enough to be permanently useful. (7) Fry's inspiration was that these adhesive might serve to keep his place temporarily in the choir book without becoming permanently **attached**—"a temporary permanent adhesive," as Fry put it.

(8) When Fry came to work on Monday and began making his bookmarks, it didn't take long before they began to envision other uses for him. (9) He realized the notes were a systematic approach to note making, because it had a built-in means of attachment and removal. (10) The idea was not an instant success, however. (11) The adhesive had to be modified slightly to make it temporary enough and permanent enough, and these took quite a bit of experimentation.

Notes:

Slightly adapted from Royston M. Roberts, *Serendipity: Accidental Discoveries in Science*, New York: Wiley, 1989.

scraps (of paper) small, irregular pieces of paper
adhesive a material that sticks to something else
discard throw away
attached fasten on to, affix to, or connect

Post-it® Fax Note 7671 | Date | # of pages ▶
To | From
Co./Dept. | Co.
Phone # | Phone #
Fax # | Fax #

Activity 6

Partners. Read the following proverbs and sayings:

- Necessity is the mother of invention.
- Never put off until tomorrow what you can do today.
- The early bird catches the worm.
- An idle mind is the devil's playground.
- Success is nine-tenths perspiration and one-tenth inspiration.

IT WORKS!
Learning Strategy:
Paying Attention to
Your Ideas

1. What do these proverbs and sayings mean?
2. What attitude do they communicate about work and success?
3. Are there similar proverbs in your own language? Think of at least three examples from your country.

If possible, work with a partner from a different cultural background and answer the preceding questions. Together, write up your responses to the questions. After writing, check your use of pronouns for clear reference.

Activity 7

Partners. Write about one or two inventions or discoveries that you could not do without and explain why. Exchange papers with a partner and discuss your ideas and your use of ties between sentences (articles, other determiners, and pronouns).

Lesson 22: Ties across Sentences

Repetitions and Transition Words

PREVIEW

In 1945, women over 16 made up more than one-third (35.8 percent) of the U.S. work force. However, by 1990, women made up more than half (57.5 percent), and in the year 2000 they are expected to comprise nearly two-thirds (62.6 percent). However, unlike Betty Crocker, some advertisers' images of women have not kept up with their changing—and often multiple—roles.

Source: General Mills. Published in *The Wall Street Journal.* April 24, 1995. Reprinted by permission.

Betty Crocker through the Years.

FOR YOUR INFORMATION Betty Crocker is a fictitious home economist created by General Mills to give the impression that one person, rather than a staff of home economists, was answering customers' questions. Today Betty Crocker symbolizes General Mills' commitment to service and quality of its convenience foods and other products.

Answer these questions and discuss your answers with a partner:

1. How are women portrayed (represented in pictures and in words) in advertising? Think of recent ads you have seen in magazines, in newspapers, on TV, and on billboards.
2. How are men portrayed in advertising? Do you see any differences between the images of men and women?

PRESENTATION

Lesson 21 focused on making ties across sentences with articles, other determiners (*this/that, another/the other/other*), and pronouns. This lesson focuses on two other ways of making ties between sentences: (1) repetition and (2) transition words and phrases. The underlined words in the Preview are examples of repetition and transition words.

Repetition is the use of repeated words and phrases. When used effectively, repetition can help the listener or reader make connections between sentences and ideas in a text. But when overused, repetition can become boring and even annoying.

Transition words and phrases, like coordinators, are used to combine independent clauses. But they are more specific than coordinators in how they relate the ideas in two independent clauses. Table 6.2 lists common transition words and phrases. For a more detailed list, see *The Tapestry Grammar,* Chapter 4, Figure 4-2, pages 68–69.

TABLE 6.2 Common Transition Words and Phrases

actually	finally	in fact
additionally*	first	in summary*
also	for example	likewise
apparently	for instance	moreover*
as a result*	for this reason	next
at any rate	fortunately	nevertheless*
besides	furthermore*	on the other hand
certainly	however*	similarly*
consequently*	in addition	then
even so	in brief	therefore*
eventually	in contrast*	thus*

*Used mainly in formal writing.

Punctuating transition words/phrases. Review the following patterns and guidelines for punctuating transition words/phases.

(SP = Subject + Predicate; T = Transition words [underlined]):

1. **SP. T, SP.**
During World War II, many women entered the U.S. work force. As a result, Rosie the Riveter, a woman working in a munitions factory, became a popular image.
2. **SP; T, SP.**
In 1945 women made up more than one-third of the work force; nowadays, women make up nearly 60 percent.
3. Transition words usually have commas after them; very short transition words (e.g., *then, next, thus*) may not.
4. When a transition word interrupts a clause, it is preceded and followed by a comma: After World War II, many women left their jobs to return home. By 1951, however, more women were working than in 1945.

Table 6.3 lists coordinators, transition words and phrases, and subordinators that are related in meaning.

TABLE 6.3 Coordinators and Subordinators with Similar Meanings

MEANING	COORDINATORS	TRANSITION WORDS AND PHRASES	SUBORDINATORS
Contrasting	but yet	even so however* in contrast* in spite of that instead nevertheless* on the contrary* on the other hand otherwise still	although even though though
Concluding/ Stating a reason	so for	accordingly* as a result* as a/in consequence* consequently* in conclusion* for this reason hence* therefore* thus* to conclude*	because since
Adding	and	additionally* also besides furthermore* in addition in the same way likewise moreover* similarly	

*Used mainly in formal writing

LEARNING STRATEGY

Forming Concepts: Using color-coded cards can help you learn important distinctions between related groups of words.

PRACTICE

Activity 1

Partners/Groups. Refer to Table 6.2 on page 129, and then complete the activity.

With a partner or in a group, divide the transition words or phrases in the table into the eight categories that are listed. An example is given in each of the categories. In a few cases, the same transition word or phrase can occur in more than one category. Check your work with a partner or your group. Then compare your answers to Chapter 4, Figure 4-2, pages 68–69 in *The Tapestry Grammar*.

ADDING	CONTRASTING	CONCLUDING
in addition	*in contrast*	*as a result*

COMPARING	ADDING DETAIL	SUMMARIZING
similarly	*for example*	*in summary*

INDICATING SEQUENCE	EXPRESSING OPINION
first	*actually*

LEARNING STRATEGY

Overcoming Limitations: Checking with a native speaker helps you ensure that you understand small differences in meaning.

Activity 2

Partners. Read about how women have been portrayed in advertising from World War II to the 1990s. Add an appropriate transition word or phrase in the blanks from the suggested category. Remember that not all transition words or phrases in a category are interchangeable; even transitions that are similar in meaning have subtle differences between them. Compare your answers with a partner and discuss any differences in your choices.

FOR YOUR INFORMATION Ask a classmate or your teacher if you don't know what the following companies produce: Pillsbury, Polaroid, Maidenform.

(1) During World War II, more and more women entered the U.S. work force to fuel the needs of a wartime economy. (2) ______________ (1 (adding detail)), the number of working women peaked at 19 million in 1944. (3) During that time, many advertisers portrayed women in their expanded roles: in military uniforms, in slacks, and in kitchen aprons.

(4) ______________ (2 (contrasting)), by late 1944, women were being prepared to give up their jobs when the soldiers returned home. (5) According to one professor, "Advertisers made a decision about what the world would be like after the war." (6) They began showing women at home again, sometimes implying that a working mother was bad for children. (7) In one advertisement, ______________ (3 (adding detail)) a young child asked, "Mother, when will you stay home again?"

(8) In the 1950s, most advertisers portrayed women as housewives and mothers, despite the fact that the number of working women had again increased to more than 19 million. (9) ______________________ (4 (adding detail)), in one Pillsbury commercial for hash browns, a woman coos, "It's a real pleasure to cook for an appreciative man." (10) Women continued to be shown in traditional roles throughout most of the 1960s.

(11) By the end of the 1970s, 50 percent of American women were at work. (12) ______________________ (5 (concluding)), it was time for advertisers to reevaluate how they thought about women. (13) Memorable ads from the 1970s included a Polaroid ad featuring actors Mariette Hartley and James Garner where Ms. Hartley was shown fixing a car.

(14) The 1980s, ______________________ (6 (contrasting)), produced some misguided attempts to portray career women and supermoms, showing what a struggle it was for advertisers to blend the traditional and new roles for women. (15) Many women, ______________________ (7 (adding detail)), still **bristle** at a perfume ad showing a woman who can "bring home the bacon, fry it up in a pan, and never, never let you forget you're a man." (16) Despite the reference to making money, "women [in the 1980s] were still judged by their ability to attract a man," according to Kimberly Barta, of the American Advertising Museum in Portland, Oregon.

(17) By the 1990s, major changes were being made in how women were treated in advertising. (18) One of the most revolutionary changes came from Maidenform, Inc., which gave up showing women in bras for more political and social messages. (19) Portrayals of women still aren't perfect, say advertising executives, particularly in predominantly male-dominated fields such as insurance, mutual funds, and business travel. (20) ______________________ (8 (contrasting)), as Marlena Pelio-Lazar, a senior advertising executive, notes, "We are better at not just offering a one-dimensional characteristic of women."

Adapted from Fara Warner, "Imperfect Picture" [Special Section: War's End], *Wall Street Journal,* April 24, 1995.

bristle become irritated, be distrubed

Activity 3

Individuals/Groups. Although all transition words and phrases can occur at the beginning of an independent clause, only some can occur in the middle of a clause, as in the sentence:

Many women, in fact, still bristle at a perfume ad from the 1980s.

On your own, read two or three articles from a newspaper, a popular magazine, or a newsletter on any topic. Make a list of any transition words or phrases that can interrupt a clause. Write the sample sentence you found using the transition word or phrase. As a group, compare your list of transition words and phrases with others. You may want to combine your individual lists into one to share with everyone.

Activity 4

The passage in Activity 2 contains many **repetitions** of the word *advertiser* as well as several **near repetitions** (related word forms, e.g., *advertise*). Circle all the repetitions and near repetitions of *advertiser* (not the first occurrence of the word).

1. How many repetitions did you find? ________
2. How many *different* near repetitions did you find? ________
   List them in the order in which they appear: ________________________________

   ____
3. There is only one **synonym** (a word that is very similar in meaning to another word) for *advertisement* in the passage. What is it? ________________________________
4. Opinion: Why do you think there are many more repetitions and near repetitions of *advertiser* than synonyms? ________________________________

   ____

Activity 5

Partners. Since World War II, more women have entered the labor force and both men and women are living longer. The following article, which reports on "the graying of America," has been changed so that it uses excessive repetition. Read the article and replace the underlined repetitions with near repetitions, pronouns, or synonyms. Some are listed for you after the article. Compare your answers with a partner's.

Americans 65 or older play 32 percent of all rounds of golf, take 72 percent of all recreational vehicle trips, and make up 60 percent of all vacation cruise passengers. And nearly 34 million Americans—one in eight—have reached or passed their 65th birthday, according to a report released today by the Population Reference Bureau, Inc.

The number of <u>Americans 65 or older</u>[1] quadrupled during the first half of the twentieth century, the research organization said. By the middle of the twenty-first century, roughly one in five, or 80 million people, will be 65 or older, the report said.

"In one way or another every institution in American society has had to accommodate the needs of <u>Americans 65 or older</u>[2], win their favor, or mobilize their resources and contributions," said Judith Treas, the report's author and professor of sociology at the University of California, Irvine.

The report said that Florida has the highest percentage of <u>Americans 65 or older</u>[3], with 18.4 percent; followed by Pennsylvania, 15.9 percent; Rhode Island, 15.5 percent; and Iowa and West Virginia, each with 15.4 percent. Alaska had the smallest share, with 4.6 percent of its population <u>65 or older</u>[4]. The number of Americans age 100 or older more than tripled to 52,000 from 1980 to 1995, the report said. That number may reach one million by the middle of the twenty-first century.

Most <u>Americans 65 and older</u>[5] report having at least one chronic health problem. Heart disease, for example, is reported by nearly one-third. Almost half are troubled by arthritis.

One of every eight <u>Americans 65 and older</u>[6] is poor, the report said. Although poverty is no longer endemic among <u>Americans 65 and older</u>[7]—as it was 40 years ago—it is a reality for 12 percent of <u>Americans 65 and older</u>[8], 28 percent of older African Americans, and 21 percent of elderly Hispanics. Social Security remains the biggest single source of income for <u>Americans 65 and older</u>[9], accounting for two of every five dollars <u>Americans 65 and older</u>[10] receive, the report said.

Adapted from "34 Million Americans Have Reached 65th Birthday," *Beloit Daily News,* April 27, 1995.

elderly Americans	senior citizens	elderly	older Americans
older people	the elderly	seniors	elderly Americans

1. In addition to <u>Americans 65 and older</u>, what other phrase or clause is repeated too much?
2. How could you change the repeated words in (1) to avoid the repetition?

Activity 6.

Everyone is an expert at something. Think of a procedure, an activity, or a product that you make or do well (and you would like to share with others).

1. Make a list of transition words or phrases that indicate sequence in time (e.g., *first, second, next*). Refer to *The Tapestry Grammar,* Chapter 4, Figure 4-2, pages 68–69, for a more detailed list.
2. Describe the steps you take to complete the procedure, activity, or product, using appropriate sequence signals.
3. Share your description with a partner and comment on each other's descriptions and use of sequence signals.

Lesson 23: Asking Questions

An Overview of Question Types

PREVIEW

In March 1995, a poll that surveyed attitudes on social, political, and economic issues was conducted in Japan, Germany, and the United States. The findings on one question are presented in Table 6.4.

TABLE 6.4 A Sample of Opinion

In the following list of items, indicate how satisfied you are in each area:	**UNITED STATES**	**GERMANY**	**JAPAN**
Your job security			
More satisfied	52%	46%	15%
Less satified	28%	24%	71%
Your income keeping up with the cost of living			
More satisfied	42%	37%	13%
Less satisfied	56%	59%	82%
Your ability to retire financially secure			
More satisfied	38%	54%	10%
Less satisfied	58%	40%	75%
The cost of housing			
More satisfied	49%	57%	20%
Less satisfied	46%	39%	59%
The cost and coverage of your health care			
More satisfied	50%	55%	15%
Less satisfied	47%	41%	78%

Source: Based on "A Sampling of Opinion," a sample of items from a survey conducted for *The Wall Street Journal,* April 24, 1995, in partnership with *Nihon Keizai Shimbun* in Japan and *Handelsblatt* in Germany.

1. Write two questions about Table 6.4 that you have to answer with "Yes" or "No."

___

___

2. Write two questions about Table 6.4 that you have to answer with specific information.

___

___

3. Check with a partner to see whether your questions are correct; then ask each other your questions.

PRESENTATION

You probably wrote examples of two types of questions in the Preview: Yes/No questions and *Wh-* information questions. In addition to these two types of questions, this lesson reviews and practices two other types: rising intonation questions and tag questions.

Table 6.5 gives information about the first three types of questions. The fourth type, tag questions, are discussed later.

TABLE 6.5 Question Types and Examples

QUESTION TYPE	CHARACTERISTICS	EXAMPLES
Yes/No Affirmative	Begin with an auxiliary (BE, DO, HAVE, or MODAL); usually answered "Yes" or "No"	End with rising intonation: • Are you self-employed? • Do you have health insurance?
Negative	Usually answered negatively	• Can't you get insurance? Expected answer: • No, I can't.
***Wh-* information** Not about subject	Begin with *wh*-word (or how) followed by auxiliary + subject + predicate	Usually end with falling intonation: • Where do you work? • When did you start?
About subject	Begin with *wh*-word (= subject) followed by predicate	• Who works with you? • Who supervises you?
Intonation Only Yes/No	Begin with a statement; used in informal settings	End with rising intonation: • You don't like the hours?
Wh- information	Begin with a word or statement followed by *wh-word;* informal, used when you have not heard all the information correctly	• You work how long? • The job ended when?

PRACTICE

Activity 1

Practice with question formation (Partners). Look over the responses to the following survey questions in Table 6.6. Then, for each of the pairs of sentences, write a question that goes with the answer. Compare your questions with a partner's questions. The first one is done for you.

TABLE 6.6 A Sample of Opinion on the Economy

	UNITED STATES	GERMANY	JAPAN
Which of the following countries do you think currently has the strongest overall economy?			
Japan	37%	48%	31%
Germany	15%	22%	12%
United States	37%	16%	38%
Which country do you think will have the strongest economy 10 years from now?			
Japan	26%	26%	13%
Germany	12%	19%	7%
United States	43%	11%	17%
Russia	1%	1%	1%
China	11%	17%	55%
Other	—	3%	2%
Not sure	7%	23%	5%
Among these same countries, which do you think generally makes the best-quality products?			
Japan	29%	17%	78%
Germany	17%	69%	14%
United States	47%	3%	3%
Russia	—	—	—
China	2%	1%	1%
Other	1%	1%	1%
Not sure	4%	9%	3%

Source: Based on "A Sampling of Opinion," sample items from a survey conducted for *The Wall Street Journal,* April 24, 1995.

NOTE The answers to the following questions are based on the response with the highest percentage from the United States, Germany, and Japan (top row).

1. Q: *Which country does Germany think has the strongest economy today?*
   A: Germany (48%) thinks Japan has the strongest economy today.
2. Q: __________
   A: No, Japan thinks the United States has the strongest economy.
3. Q: __________
   A: The United States is evenly divided between Japan and itself.
4. Q: __________
   A: Germany thinks Japan will still have the strongest economy 10 years from now.
5. Q: __________
   A: Japan thinks China will have the strongest economy in 10 years.
6. Q: __________
   A: No, the United States doesn't agree with Japan.
7. Q: __________
   A: Only one country thinks the United States will have the strongest economy in 10 years: the United States

8. Q: ______________________________

A: No, no country agrees on which country makes the best-quality products.

9. Q: ______________________________

A: Not surprisingly, each country thinks its own products are generally the best.

10. Q: ______________________________

A: Maybe because people in each country are loyal to their own country and the products it makes.

11. Q: ______________________________

A: Yes, all three countries agreed on something—no country mentioned Russia as a producer of best-quality products.

Activity 2

Have attitudes toward the world's political systems changed since World War II? Read the following simple and humorous definitions of the different political systems in the world during the World War II era and match the definitions with the political system. Then, without looking at each other's answers, ask a partner questions to find out whether your answers agree. If you disagree on answers, ask each other why.

FOR YOUR INFORMATION The New Deal refers to programs for economic recovery, reform, and social security that were introduced during the 1930s by U.S. President Franklin D. Roosevelt and his administration.

1. _____ You have two cows. The government takes one and gives it to your neighbor because he doesn't have a cow.	**a.** Capitalism
2. _____ You have two cows. The government takes both and gives you the milk.	**b.** Communism
3. _____ You have two cows. The government takes both and sells you the milk.	**c.** Fascism
4. _____ You have two cows. The government takes both and shoots you.	**d.** Nazism
5. _____ You have two cows. The government takes both and shoots one, milks the other, and throws the milk away.	**e.** New Deal
6. _____ You have two cows. You sell one and buy a bull.	**f.** Socialism

From *Wisconsin State Journal,* June 27, 1993. Knight-Ridder Newspapers.
Originally published in a FDR-era farm journal in the United States.

Activity 3

Partners. Think back to this date: **November 9, 1989.** Ask another person questions related to this date beginning with the first question. Use rising intonation questions as appropriate.

1. Where were you on November 9, 1989?
2. (You didn't hear the place correctly.) You were . . .
3. What were you . . .
4. Why were you . . .
5. Who were you . . .
6. (You didn't hear the people correctly.) You were . . .

Now ask your partner:

1. Have you ever been to Germany?
2. Have you even been to Berlin?
3. Did you know that Berlin was divided into East and West Berlin after World War II?
4. Have you ever stopped at the Brandenburg Gates in Berlin?

If you have, then you've been to the site of the Berlin Wall, built in 1961 to divide East and West Berlin. November 9, 1989, marks the celebration of the fall of the Berlin Wall.

Activity 4

Read the following information about tag questions and then complete the activity. Tag questions are mainly used when the speaker expects either a "Yes" or "No" answer or when the speaker is looking for agreement or confirmation. Tag questions start with a statement and end with a short "Yes" or "No" question. Both form and intonation are important in constructing and understanding tag questions.

TABLE 6.7 Basic Information about Tag Questions

TYPES OF TAG QUESTIONS	CHARACTERISTICS	EXAMPLES
Positive	If the statement is positive, the tag is negative; the pronoun in the tag agrees with the subject in the statement	**You've** been to New York before, **haven't you?**
Negative	If the statement is negative, the tag is positive; the pronoun in the tag agrees with the subject in the statement	**You haven't** been to the United Nations before, **have you?**
Rising intonation	Indicates a polite request for information; answer could be yes or no	The tour is at 1:00 P.M., isn't it? Answer: Yes, it is/No, it isn't.
	Softens a request (positive statement with a positive tag)	Give me a bus schedule, would you?
Falling intonation	Speaker expects the answer to agree with the statement (not the tag) or confirm that the statement is true	Inviting participation: It's a great day for a tour, isn't it? Expected answer: Yes, it is.
	Tone can range from polite (inviting participation) to impolite (discouraging participation, accusing, insulting)	Accusing: You weren't listening again, were you? Expected answer: No, I wasn't.

Tag questions can vary along a continuum from polite to impolite, depending on intonation and other voice features. See *The Tapestry Grammar,* Chapter 2, pages 21–26 and pages 30–32, for more information.

LEARNING STRATEGY

Overcoming Limitations: Asking a native speaker to show how a change in pronunciation affects meaning can help you master tag questions.

Two friends are having a rather odd conversation in New York City. Complete the tag question for each of the following statements. Remember to add a question mark at the end of each question.

FOR YOUR INFORMATION When there is more than one verb in the statement, remember that the auxiliary in the tag corresponds to the main verb. With compound pronouns (e.g., *everything, something, everybody, no one*), use *it* (for things) and *they* (for people) in the tag.

1. You've seen the new dinosaur exhibit at the Museum of Natural History, ______________________

2. That's at Central Park West and 81st Street, ______________________

3. You don't think I would go there, ____________

4. Why not? Kids aren't the only ones who like dinosaur bones, ____________

5. I guess not. A lot of adults saw the film *Jurassic Park,* ____________

6. Yeah. But the dinosaurs in that movie actually moved, ____________

7. You're right. But maybe dinosaurs aren't really dead. Everybody's been saying that birds are modern-day dinosaurs, ____________

8. Not *everybody*. A few of us think that Gila monsters are more related to dinosaurs, ____________

Gila monster a poisonous lizzard covered with black and yellowish scales that is found in the southwestern United States

Activity 5

Read the following tag questions aloud using the intonation that is marked. Then, in column **(A),** say whether the speaker expects a certain answer or not, and in **(B),** say what the expected answer is.

TAG QUESTION	(A) Does the speaker expect a certain answer?	(B) If (A) is yes, what answer is expected?
1. Birds are related to dinosaurs, aren't they?	______	____________
2. You've heard of that theory, haven't you?	______	____________
3. You don't read the newspapers, do you?	______	____________
4. You'd rather watch TV and drink beer, wouldn't you?	______	____________
5. I prefer watching the news on TV instead of reading it, don't I?	______	____________
6. Let's change the subject, shall we?	______	____________

Source: Based on an exercise in H. Riggenbach and V. Samuda, *Grammar Dimensions: Form, Meaning, and Use 2.* Boston: Heinle & Heinle, 1993.

LEARNING STRATEGY

Managing Your Learning: Using the context can help you guess an answer.

Activity 6

Partners. What is it? Study the picture and then complete the question or answer in each pair of sentences. In most of the sentences, more than one response is possible.

1. Q: ______________________

   A: Anybody can use it.
2. Q: ______________________

   A: It's been available for about five years.
3. Q: ______________________

   A: People often use it before they eat a certain kind of food.
4. Q: ______________________

   A: It's made of plastic.
5. Q: ______________________

   A: It costs less than $5.00.
6. Q: It's been advertised on TV, hasn't it?

   A: ______________________
7. Q: ______________________

   A: No, but a patent is pending.
8. Q: ______________________

   A: You can get it from Tony's Pizza!

See the end of the chapter for the answer.

Based on an idea by Ilyse Rathet Post.

Activity 7

Groups. You've just met someone at an airport. Both of you have two hours to kill until your plane leaves. When you meet someone for the first time in North America, what are some questions you might ask? As a group, develop a list of questions and then decide which are acceptable and which are unacceptable to North Americans.

Lesson 24: Asking Questions

Full and Reduced Forms

PREVIEW

How many of these questions have you heard before? Circle the number of any question that you have been asked.

1. Where are you from?
2. What are you doing here?
3. How long have you studied English?
4. Where do you live?
5. Do you like it?
6. Is this your first time here?

Write down any other questions that you are frequently asked:

____

____

____

____

____

PRESENTATION

Questions 1 to 6 in the Preview are written in standard, full forms. In informal speech, these questions can also be asked using reduced forms. One way to form reduced questions is to contract the auxiliary to a *wh*-word:

QUESTION WORD	SUBJECT	PREDICATE
How long've	you	studied English?
Where'd	you	learn it?
How'd	they	teach languages there?

Sometimes, it is difficult to hear the auxiliary in past tense questions or with expanded verbs, but some form is present, even if it is reduced.

Another way to form reduced questions is to omit the auxiliary:

QUESTION WORD	MISSING AUXILIARY	SUBJECT	PREDICATE
Where	[are]	you	from?
What	[are]	you	doing here?
Where	[do]	you	live?
	[Do]	you	like it?
	[Is]	this	your first time here?
How long	[are]	you	going to stay?

Although you will sometimes hear native speakers asking *wh*-questions without auxiliaries in casual speech, omitting an auxiliary is not acceptable in formal speech, writing, or in many informal situations.

PRACTICE

Activity 1

Partners. In the following dialogue, underline all the (1) reduced questions and (2) rising intonation questions. Write the standard, full form of each question you underlined at the end. (You should find eight.) Compare your responses with a partner's.

FOR YOUR INFORMATION The Monterey Bay Aquarium, Monterey, California, is located inside the borders of the largest U.S. marine **sanctuary.** It is famous for its a three-story **kelp** forest tank, home to the sea otter and other Northern Californian marine animals.

Guide: The **kelp** forests of Monterey Bay are essential to the habitat of the sea otter. Because where there is kelp, there are sea otters.

Tourist 1: You mean the sea otters eat the kelp?

Guide: No. Sea otters depend on kelp, a type of very large seaweed, for protection against the high waves and severe weather in the ocean. They eat other creatures who also live in the kelp forests—clams, shrimp, and their favorite, sea urchins.

Tourist 2: Sea what?

Guide: Sea urchins. Their soft bodies are enclosed in a hard shell with spines, so the otters have to break them open.

Tourist 3: What do they use to break open the shells?

Guide: This is one of the most fascinating things about sea otters. They often use a small rock to break them open.

Tourist 4: How they going to do that?

Guide: Well, they float on their backs, hold the sea urchin with one front paw and break it open with the other.

Tourist 1: You mean they use rocks as a tool?

Guide: Exactly. We aren't the only animals who use tools.

Tourist 2: Where'd they get that idea? To use tools, I mean.

Guide: It's hard to say. Probably trial and error, and for the young ones, from their mothers.

Tourist 3: Don't the fathers teach the young how to hunt?

Guide: Not in otter society. The mothers raise the young and teach them how to hunt and protect themselves from predators.

Tourist 2: [to Tourist 3] Where you been? You see a lot of that kind of mothering with other animals. Birds, for example.

Tourist 3: You ever seen Canada geese? The male and female stick together for life. They both help raise the chicks.

Tourist 2: *Goslings*. Hey, where's everybody gone? We've lost the guide.

sanctuary a refuge, a protected area
kelp a type of very large, brown seaweed

1. ______________________________

2. ______________________________

3. ______________________________

4. ______________________________

5. ______________________________

6. ______________________________

7. ______________________________

8. ______________________________

Activity 2

Partners. Not all questions can be reduced from their standard, full forms by omitting the auxiliary. For example, some very short questions with pronouns cannot be reduced this way:

- Full: Where is my map? or Where is it?
- Reduced: Where's my map?
  NOT: Where it? or Where's it?
- Full: How are you?
  Reduced: How're you?
  NOT: How you?

Refer to the questions you wrote in the Preview. If possible, rewrite your questions in reduced form. Check your reduced questions with a partner or a native speaker of English.

1. ______________________________
2. ______________________________
3. ______________________________
4. ______________________________
5. ______________________________

Activity 3

Groups. Inside and outside of the classroom, it's easy to misunderstand other people. What are some ways to ask people to repeat what they have said? As a group, come up with a list of questions and then rate them from 1 to 5, where 1 is the most polite or indirect and 5 is the most impolite or direct. Compare your questions and ratings to those of another group or the class.

FOR YOUR INFORMATION It's possible to be direct with close friends and family members without being perceived as impolite. Polite-impolite and indirect-direct represent two separate continua:

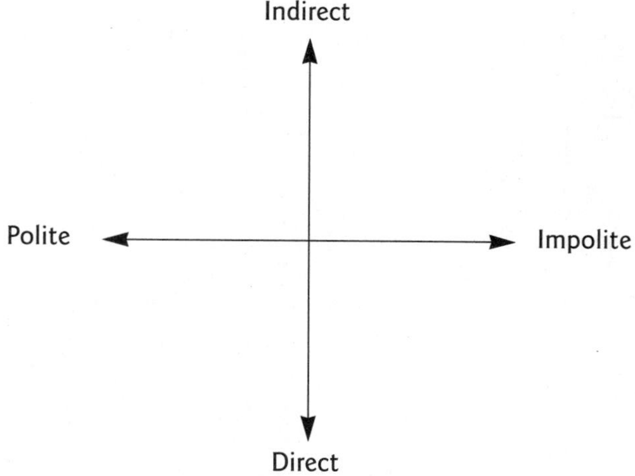

Activity 4

Groups. Bring to class a postcard that you have received from another country. One member of your group has to reproduce the information on the back of the postcard (except for the message) in the space provided below, without looking at it, by asking questions about it. Another member should write down all of the questions that are asked. When you are finished, compare the information one of you has written with the information on the postcard. Then, as a group, review your questions and make any changes needed to correct them. Mark any reduced questions, rising intonation questions, or tag questions with an asterisk (*).

Date (optional) ________________
Greeting/Name (optional)

____

TO

____

____

____

____

ANSWER TO ACTIVITY 6 IN LESSON 23 It's a new design for a pizza cutter.